£4=   7.5.T81 .

RHETORIC

AND

ENGLISH COMPOSITION

BY

HERBERT J. C. GRIERSON

LL.D., LITT.D., LITT. ET PHIL.D.

PROFESSOR-EMERITUS OF RHETORIC AND ENGLISH
LITERATURE, UNIVERSITY OF EDINBURGH

Ce n'est pas assez de savoir la Théologie pour
écrire de la Théologie : il faut encore savoir écrire,
qui est une seconde science.

JEAN-LOUIS GUEZ DE BALZAC (1597-1664)
"Grand Épistolier de France."

SECOND EDITION—REVISED

OLIVER AND BOYD LTD.

EDINBURGH: TWEEDDALE COURT
LONDON: 98 GREAT RUSSELL STREET, W.C.

1945

First Published	September 1944
Second Edition—Revised	May 1945
Reprinted	November 1945

PRINTED AND PUBLISHED IN GREAT BRITAIN BY
OLIVER AND BOYD LTD., EDINBURGH

PREFACE

In the month of June 1893 the present writer was examined at Oxford in the school of *Litteræ Humaniores*, learning the result in the following August. On 30th September of the same year he was appointed to give a course of one hundred lectures to the class of English Literature in the University of Aberdeen. It was an interim appointment for the months in which an ordinance founding a new Chair was lying before Parliament. Five lectures were to be delivered every week, beginning on or about the 15th of October.

It was rather a staggering proposition, and I slept little for a week or more. Of University teaching in English I had enjoyed just fifty lectures at Aberdeen, of which twenty-five were devoted to Rhetoric or, as Rhetoric had come to mean under Dr Alexander Bain and his successor William Minto, English Composition. I had at school been drilled in Bain's *Higher English Grammar* (1863, 1879), and I had used his first *English Composition and Rhetoric: A Manual* (1866) while teaching in a school between my years at Aberdeen and Oxford. Moreover, I had just been studying the *Nicomachean Ethics* of Aristotle under the late John A. Stewart, then tutor at Christ Church, later White's Professor of Moral Philosophy in the University. It was thus a relief to know that I might begin my course by lecturing on Rhetoric for a few weeks, and so give myself more time to get ready for the formidable task of tracing the history of English Literature.

I have mentioned the *Ethics* of Aristotle because the benefit I had got from that work suggested to me to examine the *Rhetoric* which was no longer studied at Oxford, as I gather it had once been, having picked up a copy of Becker's text (1831) interleaved and fully, or almost fully, annotated from a tutor's lectures or lessons by a " H. Anstey e Coll. Univ. Oxon. A.D. 1848." I read accordingly the article by Jebb in the Encyclopaedia, the

Aristotle of Grote, and the translation by Welldon, not having time to wrestle with the Greek text. I was struck at once with two things, the exactness with which Aristotle defined and adhered to his purpose, and secondly, the wide significance of the sentence which I have placed at the head of my second chapter. The widening of the study of Rhetoric to include much more than the orator's aim of persuasion has led to some forgetfulness of what had been Aristotle's theme ; and also to a tendency to forget the relative character of all our rules for composition— whether for the right choice of words, the correctness of our grammar, our use or disuse of figures, and everything else. One may hear Milton's style depreciated by comparison with Dryden's without any consideration whether in Dryden's style Milton could have given the tone he wished to his work or appealed to the readers he had in mind. Of Aristotle's work the late Professor Saintsbury spoke as though it were a kind of *Prosaics* meant to balance the *Poetics*, spoiled a little by the unfortunate preoccupation of the Greeks with the spoken word. But Aristotle's definition is quite clear and explicit. Rhetoric is the " faculty of discovering all the means of persuasion in any subject," and the various means, argumentative, emotional, moral, are just as applicable to poetry as to prose. Indeed, his examples are more often taken from poetry, dramatic and epic, than from prose, and in the *Poetics*, when he comes to the subject of *dianoia*, " thought," he refers the reader at once to the *Rhetoric* : " Under thought is included every effect which has to be produced by speech : in particular proof and refutation, the exciting of the feelings such as pity, fear, anger, and the like." Think of the speech by Antony in *Julius Cæsar*—its specious arguments, its suggestion of the trust-worthiness of the speaker's character :

> I am no orator, as Brutus is ;

and the final rising appeal to the emotions of the mob. If then our aim is not persuasion our methods must vary. Cicero defines the perfect orator as " qui dicendo animos audientium et docet, et delectat, et permovet," and that will cover a great deal. Yet one must observe that each of these aims will be affected if the main aim is to persuade. The definition of Quintilian—" Dicere secundum virtutem orationis. Scientia bene dicendi "—is a little vague but is accepted by Campbell in a work I will mention, and translated or paraphrased as " The art or talent by which the discourse is adapted to its end," which is sound, if it omits the subject and the audience. I should prefer to define, if that is necessary, Rhetoric as the study of how to express oneself most correctly and effectively, bearing in mind the nature of the language we use, the subject we are speaking or writing about, the kind of audience (often only vaguely definable) we have in view, and the purpose, which last is the main determinant.

Aberdeen has a long tradition of teaching Rhetoric, or had, for I do not know how far it is still maintained. Professor Dover Wilson has declared recently that " our university departments of English are in the main departments for the training of literary critics, and pay far too little attention to the student's own power of expression." That was not the main theme of the English class taught by Professor Alexander Bain; and even under his successor the lectures till Christmas were confined to Grammar and Composition with a sprinkling of Philology. The Chair which both these occupied taught the three subjects that composed the mediæval *trivium*—Grammar, Rhetoric and Logic. The last had become the main theme, and was taught, with some psychology, in a full course of one hundred lectures. Rhetoric had been hived off to a class of fifty lectures and was beginning to include some study of English Literature. A separate Chair of English Literature, including Scottish, was founded by Mr John Gray Chalmers in 1893, and I was the first occupant. But I continued to lecture on Rhetoric; and in Edinburgh the Chair was entitled " of Rhetoric and English Literature." Nor, to tell the truth, did I regard my work on the latter subject as solely concerned to make literary critics, though of course we did deal critically with certain prescribed books. Rightly or wrongly, I myself thought of it as a chapter in the history of culture, supplying something which the class of History could not comprise, being so largely concerned with constitutional changes and foreign relations. It was in the English class that I myself first got some inkling of what was meant by the Middle Ages and the adjective "mediæval"; what was meant by the Renaissance, the *Aufklärung*, the Romantic Revival, etc. But that is another question. To return to Rhetoric; as long ago as 1666 there appeared at Aberdeen :

Rudimentorum
R H E T O R I C O R U M
Libri quinque

Auctore
ROBERTO BRUNO
Presbytero Scoto.

Composed in Latin, it is dedicated : " Jacobo Bardaeo Equiti ab Auchmedden Ditionis Banfaeensis Praetori dignissimo Urbisque Banfiae Praefecto clarissimo." The first book deals with the Matter of Rhetoric, the second with Invention, the third with Disposition, the fourth with Elocution (including tropes or figures of speech), the fifth with Pronunciation. The tropes in the fourth book are defined with Scholastic precision : " Tropus est igitur quadruplex, vel enim est inter res quarum altera est de alterius essentia, quae est Synecdoche : vel si altera non sit de alteriue essentia, sed cum essentia jungitur, ibi est Metonymia : vel si altera sit alteri similis tantum, ex ea similitudine gignitur Metaphora : Quod si oppositae sint alterum pro altero ponit Ironia." The figures of speech have always, I fear, had too great an attraction for the teachers of Rhetoric.

How far this work was used in teaching I do not know. It belongs to a time when lecturing was done chiefly in Latin. Coming to a later period, in 1776 was published (in English now) *The Philosophy of Rhetoric*, by George Campbell, a noted divine and theologian, Professor in and ultimately Principal of Marischal College, Aberdeen, a very interesting piece of work covering the whole field as embraced by the Ancients : the logic of proof, the appeal to the feelings, the characteristics of different audiences, and lastly elocution or style. Dr Bain covered the same ground except Grammar and Logic, as he had dealt with these in separate works, the latter in his two volumes on Deductive and Inductive Logic. In his final edition of *Rhetoric and Composition*, in two volumes, the first is on style—words, sentences, paragraphs, figures of speech ; the second on the " Emotional Qualities of Style," but studied not, as by Aristotle, as instruments employed by the orator to persuade, but rather by the poet to give æsthetic pleasure. I have not attempted to follow him into this wide and complicated field, as my aim is practical rather than critical, to give some hints for composition, not to endeavour to give instruction in the appreciation of poetry. That, I think, is best done, so far as it can be, in the critical reading of definite texts. But Dr Bain was a very practical teacher himself, and it is of his class method I should like to say a word, so far as I can gather that from his book *On Teaching English* (1887) and from some examination of the papers which he set while Professor. He quite explicitly disapproved of essay - writing, at least for young students, on the ground that in general it meant asking the writers to make bricks without straw. What he substituted was the critical examination of passages in the light of the instruction given : " Criticise the placing of qualifying adjuncts in the following passage ; and give the regulating principle in each case, mentioning improvements where necessary " ; " Point out improvements as regards Exposition in the following " ; " Examine for Narrative " ; " Examine for Oratory," etc., etc. So they run, and they are not by any means easy questions, but Bain had, I gathered, very definite rules, and clearness was the quality to which he attached the greatest importance. I venture to think that if the passages were well chosen and carefully graded, such a practice might be combined with independent composition. Take an essay, not a too fanciful one as by Lamb, but a clear piece of writing, emphatic and interesting. Go over it sentence by sentence, paragraph by paragraph, pointing out not only errors, if there are any, or passages that might be improved, but the merits also and how they have been achieved. Consider then with the class whether there are any other points which might have been treated under the same head. Then, a little later, set an essay to be written in class on the same theme, or one so closely akin that many of the same thoughts are available.

The subjects set for essays are too often so general that a student needs all his time to dig out something to say, instead of being able to give all his or her time to the saying of it in the best way. In a scholarship examination the theme set was one word—" Fanaticism." I was rather older than most of the candidates, and had been reading philosophy ; and I found the subject interesting. Years afterwards I met a distinguished man, head of a college, who said to me : " I remember you, for as we came out of the hall you said casually to me, ' That was an interesting subject ' ; and I had *not* thought so." On the other hand, a co-examiner and myself once set in a schools examination : " A Day in the Life of a Farmer or a Gamekeeper or some other calling " ; and we got some admirable essays. It is often said that the writing of Latin prose was a good training for writing in English. A. E. Housman did not think so, and I do not feel sure. But if it was so, may it not have been just because the subject-matter was supplied and one could give all his time to the form ? I do not care for the setting of bad sentences to correct. One should never dwell long on the bad. But the study of a whole passage, from every point of view, its excellences and its faults, followed by an attempt to go and do likewise, can be of use, and one has then a full right to criticise the result. Something of this kind was, if I remember aright, the method recommended by Ascham in his *Scholemaster* for teaching Latin prose composition. For a French master (he was actually a Pole) I used to write out a translation of one hundred lines from the French. When I gave it in he handed it back to me with the one word—" Retranslate." That was too difficult a task for a boy of eleven, but it was on the right lines. " He only," says Dr Johnson, " has a right to suppose that he can express his thoughts . . . with perspicacity or elegance, who has carefully perused the best authors, accurately noted their diversities of style, diligently selected the best modes of diction, and familiarised them by long habits of attentive practice." It is of course as an occasional lesson that I suggest this combination of criticism and composition. The student will be learning to think as well as to compose, and here the teacher of English must have the help of teachers of other subjects, especially the teachers of philosophy. I always encouraged honours students to attend at least one of the classes in Philosophy. Philosophy may solve no problems, but it does encourage the mind to examine its own activities, does help to awaken the student from his dogmatic slumbers.

The first four of these chapters were given their present form during the opening weeks of the last war. The remainder existed only in the form of notes for lectures, added to from time to time.

I have tried now to throw these chapters into consecutive order. My aim throughout has been rather to suggest a point of view than to dictate rigid rules.

I am indebted to Mr H. J. Laski and to Messrs Faber & Faber for permission to print the paragraph on pp. 119-20; and to Mr Cecil Day Lewis and Messrs Jonathan Cape for permission to print the poem on pp. 144-5.

H. J. C. G.

CONTENTS

CHAPTER I

RHETORIC IN THE ANCIENT WORLD:
ARISTOTLE

IT was among the Greek peoples of the Mediterranean that the kind of oratory took its rise which we think of when we speak of Demosthenes, Cicero, Bossuet, Jeremy Taylor, Edmund Burke, William Ewart Gladstone, oratory in which reasoning, argument, is combined with an appeal to the emotions, a certain elevation of style, and a construction, an ordering, which leads roughly from an exordium to a peroration. When Satan in Milton's *Paradise Lost* had brought Eve to the fatal tree of the knowledge of good and evil, then, the poet tells us :

> The Tempter, but with show of zeal and love
> To Man, and indignation at his wrong,
> New part puts on, and, as to passion mov'd,
> Fluctuates disturb'd, yet comely, and in act
> Rais'd, as of some great matter to begin.
> As when of old some orator, renown'd
> In Athens or free Rome, where eloquence
> Flourish'd, since mute, to some great cause addrest,
> Stood in himself collected, while each part,
> Motion, each act, won audience ere the tongue.
> Sometimes in highth began, as no delay
> Of preface brooking, through his zeal of right :
> So standing, moving, or to highth upgrown,
> The Tempter, all impassion'd, thus began.

So Milton sees the first great orator, as too often in later days, bent on misleading poor humanity. It was in Sicily apparently that the systematic study of the means of persuading a popular audience began, as a consequence of the frequency of lawsuits arising out of the political revolutions which accompanied the expulsion of the tyrants from the cities of Sicily. Suppose that you had been driven out of the city by a tyrant, you returned on the next political turn-over to find your house and property occupied by another, and it was necessary for you to prove your right to that property before an Assembly of the Citizens. You might be able to produce documents, but you might not, and your business in any case would be to persuade a set of judges who were not as technically trained as the judges of to-day. Everything would depend on your power of persuading them, whether by an appeal to the judgement or an appeal to their prejudices and feelings. A certain Corax and another, Tisias, have got the credit of being the first to undertake to teach young men the art of persuasion. Their teaching was not systematic, but consisted apparently of useful wrinkles and some instruction in style and arrangement, for very early it was perceived how much influence mere beauty of language and utterance had upon a popular audience. To this day negro audiences are enormously swayed by an eloquent flow of words. It was a certain Gorgias, known to us mainly from Plato and Aristotle, who developed this stylistic side of rhetoric and cultivated an artificial highly rhythmical prose full of poetical phrases, metaphors, strange words and long sentences with elaborately balanced clauses, the balance emphasised by the use of alliteration. Gorgias may be called the fountainhead of artistic Greek, Latin, French and English prose. He was sent to Athens in 427 B.C. as an ambassador from the city of Leontini, and he swept his audiences off their feet by the novelty and artifice of his eloquence.

"Plausibility and not Truth, Brilliance of Diction and not soundness of Argument" were, Cope[1] says, the aim of these early teachers of rhetoric, and they naturally evoked the opposition of a great teacher of Truth like Socrates, whose own method of discourse was not by a sustained oratory but consisted in a skilful use of question and answer. But the fundamental opposition between the sophists or rhetoricians on the one hand and Socrates and Plato on the other was that the ends they had in view were different. The aim of the rhetoricians was to teach the young men how by eloquence they could attain to power; that of Socrates and Plato was to teach them the way to attain to Truth. This comes out clearly in Plato's dialogue, the *Gorgias*. "Rhetoric," Gorgias there declares, "is the art of persuasion in the Courts

---

[1] *The Rhetoric of Aristotle.* With a Commentary by E. M. Cope. Revised and edited by J. E. Sandys (Cambridge, 1877).

and other Assemblies, and about the just and unjust," and he goes on to show that in every art or profession the trained orator will have more power even than the specialist in that profession. He can persuade the patient to take physic when the doctor fails to do so, and he can persuade the jury to acquit a guilty man, although, to be fair to Gorgias, he does not approve of such a misuse of his art. Still, the fact remains that rhetoric is the art of persuasion and that the success of the orator does not depend entirely, or perhaps at all, on the truth of his argument but on the manner in which he is able to present what he wishes his audience to accept as true, and that his power is greatest with an ignorant or unprofessional audience. As Cicero says later: " We [that is orators] speak to those who do not know, not knowing ourselves." To Socrates it seemed that rhetoric was not really an art but a kind of trick, " the habit of a bold and ready wit which knows how to behave in this world," a trick of flattery which stands to the true art of persuading and governing a people just as cookery does to the art of medicine. The doctor by his art is able to tell us what we ought to eat or what we ought not to eat. The cook by his craft persuades us to eat things which are *not* good for us to eat, or to eat more of them than is wise. In like manner rhetoric in the mouth of the popular politician persuades a people to do what a ruler who is seeking only truth and justice would know to be unwise or wrong.

But Plato's quarrel is not so much with the art or craft of the rhetorician as with his end. He does not believe that the power of the rhetorician is nearly so great as he himself imagines. The true corrupter of the young politician, he tells us in the *Republic*, is not the rhetorician but the people themselves demanding that they shall get what they wish whether it be wise or not to grant it. This comes out clearly in the later part of the *Gorgias*, where a younger man, Polus, takes up the theme and pleads for the utility of oratory as an instrument of power. Socrates maintains that the power thus secured is not *real* power, that a wicked man who has secured power by his rhetoric, or other illegitimate means, has not gained *real* power because he has not attained the happiness which, consciously or unconsciously, he is in quest of; and Socrates goes on to maintain the paradox that " Rhetoric is of no use to us in helping a man to excuse his own injustice, or that of his parents, or friends, or children or country ; but may be of use if we hold that, instead of excusing he ought to accuse, himself above all and in the next degree his family, or any of his friends who may be doing wrong, if he does not want to conceal but to bring to light the iniquity, that the wrongdoer may suffer and by suffering be healed."

Plato speaks as the great moral and religious prophet for whom the only true value in life is righteousness, to save one's soul. " What shall it profit a man if he gain the whole world and lose his own soul ? " Accordingly, like the Author of the Sermon on the Mount, Plato speaks in paradoxes because his values are not the world's values. Aristotle approaches the question of rhetoric in the spirit of a man of science, concerned not so much with what ought or ought not to be as with what is, which it is necessary to understand aright. Here is the fact of rhetoric, the fact that speakers can persuade by proofs of various kinds. Let us analyse it a little and find out by what means persuasion is affected. Aristotle is well aware of Plato's objections and knows that the art may be abused. A great deal of the oratory of the time is, he says, illegitimate. " Strict Justice if applicable to Rhetoric would confine itself to seeking such a delivery as would cause neither pain nor pleasure." The only thing which should be permitted to the orator in the law courts is to expound the arguments for or against the cause. He should not be allowed to make any appeal to the prejudices or emotions of his audience. But the orator *does* make such appeals, and it is necessary to examine his methods. Rhetoric may be a useful art (1) because, as Truth and Justice are naturally stronger than their opposites, if they are defeated it must be the fault of those who undertook to defend them ; (2) because there are audiences on whom strict reasoning is lost : they must be got at by easier, more popular methods, by an appeal to generally accepted notions ; (3) because if we cannot argue on both sides of a question we shall fail to recognise an unfair argument when it is used against us ; (4) because if it is honourable to be able to defend ourselves physically so also it is an accomplishment to be able to defend ourselves by speech, and (5) lastly, because it is no condemnation of any art that it may be abused. The truth is that the objection taken by Socrates and Plato to rhetoric is one of three instances in which the moralist has taken exception at once to the abstract methods of the scientist. Science always deals with its appropriate subject in an abstract manner, it ignores factors which do not strictly concern the scientist's purpose. The chemist discovers explosives, but it is not *his* business to decide whether these explosives are to be used for quarrying stone or for blowing up our fellowmen. But in certain cases it has been felt at once that such abstraction, the ignoring of moral considerations, is dangerous. Rhetoric is one instance of this ; Machiavelli's study of government in the fifteenth century was another ; and a third was the study of economics in the nineteenth century, the wealth of nations, which evoked the protest of Ruskin in *Unto this Last* and other works.

Aristotle accordingly composed a philosophical treatise on Rhetoric of which it has been said that in it a science was at once begun and finished. Aristotle's statements have indeed been expanded and illustrated by later authors, and when real oratory came to an end with the disappearance of freedom in Greece and Rome, the study of the stylistic part of rhetoric was elaborated beyond all real necessity. Rhetoric began to be in later authors merely a study of elaborate artifices of prose style. No one has added anything essential to Aristotle's treatment of the whole subject.

Aristotle holds that oratory is the art of persuading by various means an audience consisting of persons who are unable to apprehend a number of arguments in a single view, that is to say, a popular audience. There are three main " proofs," or avenues of persuasion, Aristotle points out, which the speaker makes use of. One is by the way of the intellect—that is the proofs proper, the arguments which the speaker advances to establish the truth or untruth of what is asserted, the probability or improbability of success in the policy recommended to his audience. These are in most cases the only legitimate proofs. But as a fact they are with the popular audience generally the least important, for of average human nature, as Burke declares, the reason is only a part, and often a very small part. Accordingly there are two other lines of approach—the moral and the emotional. Much in a speech depends upon what the audience thinks of the speaker himself, the impression of his own character which he succeeds in conveying. There are three qualities which he must suggest

to his audience that he possesses—sagacity, honesty, and goodwill
to his audience. That is the note which Antony strikes when he
declares :

> I am no orator, as Brutus is ;
> But, as you know me all, a plain blunt man,
> That love my friend.

The third of the orator's weapons is the appeal to the feelings,
the disposition which he induces in the audience. This was, in
ancient oratory at any rate, the greatest, the most effective weapon
of the orator whether addressing a jury or a popular assembly.
In our law courts the use of this weapon has been to some extent
restrained by tradition and by the authority of the judge. It is
difficult to imagine any agent for the Crown making such an
impassioned personal attack upon the unhappy accused as was
made in America in the prosecution of the man accused of
murdering the Lindbergh baby, or appealing to the jury by
exhibiting the infant victim's sleeping-suit. But that was quite
in the manner of Greek and Roman advocates. The accused
and his family appeared in court clad in mourning with a view to
appealing to the sympathies of the jury.

These being, then, the three main means of persuasion at the
disposal of the orator, Aristotle goes on to examine more closely
the character of each. But first he distinguishes the three fields
in which oratory is exercised, depending on the audience which
the orator is addressing and the end which he has in view. For,
he says, and this applies to other literature as well as oratory, a
speech is composed of three elements—the speaker, the subject,
and the persons addressed. The three kinds of oratory which
Aristotle distinguishes are, then, (1) forensic oratory—that is the
oratory of the law courts, concerned always with a *past* event
(did this or that actually happen ?) and having as its end, its
purpose, justice ; (2) the second is deliberative oratory, the
oratory, say, of the Houses of Parliament, or of a town council,
or of any committee concerned with legislation or administration
of any kind. Oratory of this kind has in view the *future*, what
law or regulation is to be established, and its determining end is
expediency—what is the best thing to do, what is most likely to
benefit ourselves, or, it may be, to injure our enemies. The third
kind of oratory is eulogistic, the oratory to which we are accus-

tomed when a statesman has died or retired, or a clergyman is being given a presentation. An excellent example is the eulogy of Fox by Burke at the end of his speech on the East India Bill; and I myself heard Mr Gladstone deliver at Oxford a short but perfect panegyric on Sir Robert Peel, his earliest political leader.

It is with the second of these alone, deliberative oratory, that I wish to deal shortly, with a view to showing the scientific, Greek spirit in which Aristotle writes, concerning himself not with what ought or ought not to be, but simply with the right understanding of what is; and with a view also of suggesting shortly the interest which this work has for us to-day, at least in those countries which are still free and democratic.

Taking up, then, the first kind of arguments, those which are addressed to the understanding, Aristotle points out that oratorical argument is always concerned with the probable or improbable. Where scientific proof can be obtained oratory is no longer required. The orator is discussing questions about which neither he nor his audience has certain knowledge, and what he wishes to do is to persuade this audience, starting from certain generally accepted statements or appealing to certain very striking concrete examples, to follow what he thinks is the best line to take, or at any rate that which for some reason he wishes them to take, whether it be to pass an act or a regulation, or to build a building, or to construct a road, or it may be to subscribe more generously to Foreign Missions.

To do this the orator of course needs to have knowledge of the themes in which he is going to deal. In the political orator's case these are, according to Aristotle, finance, war and peace, means of defence, supplies, and legislation. What the teacher of rhetoric has to teach is how to select from among the facts acquired in the study of these different branches, and also how to use a number of arguments that are applicable in a general way to various themes. For example, the political orator has always in view expediency, that is the happiness of the people, the good which he thinks the measure he is supporting will bring to them. What, then, is " happiness " ? what is " good " ? Well, if you wished to know scientifically or philosophically what happiness is or what is the good that we ought to aim at, Plato would send you to his *Republic*, where in ten books he has tried to convince

B

his readers or hearers that happiness is identical with righteousness ; and Aristotle would refer you in like manner to his *Ethics*,
where he too has endeavoured to discover the conditions and
constituents of true happiness. But you will cut very little ice in
a popular speech with such profound and paradoxical reflections
as are those of Plato in the *Republic* about true happiness, or
such paradoxes as are the sayings in the Sermon on the Mount—
" Blessed are the poor in spirit," etc. These are counsels how
to obtain *real* happiness, the *real* good of life. But there were
not many speeches made on these high lines, for example, in
the election preceding the Treaty of Versailles. What the orator
needs to know is not what happiness is to the saint or to the
philosopher, but what ordinary people think constitutes happiness
or what is good. Aristotle accordingly proceeds to enumerate some
of the popular conceptions of happiness ; for example, happiness
consists in the pleasantest life possible conjoined with safety ; or
happiness consists in abundance of riches with power to keep and
use them, etc., etc. Some of the constituents of happiness are
noble birth, plenty of friends, wealth, a numerous family, honour,
luck, etc., etc. So again with what is good or expedient. What
we want to know is what people think is good and expedient,
and sometimes what they think is very far from being universally
true. For example, a common notion is that everything which
is bad for our enemy must be good for us.   When after
the American War the English Government was compelled
to grant to Ireland freedom of trade with Britain and the
Colonies the merchants of Bristol were very indignant with
their member, Edmund Burke. They maintained that what
was good for Ireland must be bad for them ; and Burke
endeavoured to persuade them that this was not so : " Indeed,
Sir, England and Ireland may flourish together. The world is
large enough for us both . . . your profit and theirs must concur.
Beggary and bankruptcy are not the circumstances which invite
to an intercourse with that or with any country ; and I believe
it will be found invariably true that the superfluities of a rich
nation furnish a better object of trade than the necessities of a
poor one. It is the interest of the commercial world that wealth
should be found everywhere."

Another series of popular " topics," as Aristotle calls them, consists of generally applicable arguments concerning the relative degrees of good in things : arguments to prove that A is better than B. Bacon has written a little essay on this subject which he calls " The Colours of Good and Evil " ; but Bacon recognises clearly that the arguments are oratorical, not scientific, for he points out that in each of them there is a fallacy, *i.e.* that even if generally true they are not always so. Two of his examples are interesting. When in trouble, does it make your trouble better or worse to think that it is due to your own error ? Obviously in most cases it makes it worse, the reason being that if we ourselves are not to blame we can get some relief from thinking that we can accuse others or even perhaps complain of the injustice of God ; whereas when the evil is clearly seen to be due to our own action, then, as he says, " all strikes deadly inward and suffocateth." Nevertheless this is not *always* true, for if we reflect that our trouble is due to ourselves, then in some cases we can feel it is in our own power to redeem our fortunes. " My own hand shall do it," Scott said to those who offered to help him in his financial disaster. He felt that he had brought the evil upon himself and that it was his own duty and within his own power to repair it. Again, if we wish to arouse a feeling of interest we must give a vivid picture of what is implied. If a missionary wishes to persuade us to subscribe to his work in the field of Foreign Missions or Home Missions, he must give us a vivid detailed description of the evils which he wishes to cure. But it is not *always* wise to enter in this manner too much into detail. If you wish to excuse your conduct it is not well to give more than one reason. Bacon illustrates this by the example of the fox and the cat in Æsop's Fables. The fox described the many methods he had of escaping from the dogs, and the cat said she had but one, which was to climb a tree. Such, then, without going into further detail are the kind of arguments the orator uses over and above those which belong to the specific subject he is dealing with. They are probable arguments only, for if we could attain to scientific proof discussion would cease ; and the orator's business is to use those arguments which are most likely to appear probable to the audience he is addressing, for every audience has its own susceptibilities to special kinds of reasoning. Certain arguments appeal to some minds that are quite lost upon others.

But the appeal to the understanding—though it ought, as Aristotle fully admits, to be the chief or only line of argument—is not so in most cases. The minds of men are governed more by their emotions than by their judgment. Accordingly a practical treatise on Rhetoric as the art of persuasion must deal scientifically with the appeal to the feelings. This is the subject of the second book of the *Rhetoric*, and a very interesting piece of work it seems to me to be, and lends itself most interestingly to confirmation from the great poets and dramatists who have understood the human heart and its workings. Let me take just one or two examples. With regard to each passion Aristotle asks what is the object that evokes it, and secondly, what are the conditions in which it is most easily excited. For example, anger is defined by Aristotle as " an impulse accompanied by pain to a conspicuous revenge for a conspicuous slight." A slight is not an injury. Lord Chesterfield tells his son that a gentleman may forgive an injury but never a slight. To slight you is to treat you with contempt in some way or other, to treat you as though you were a person of no importance, and to do so conspicuously, that is to say in the eyes of others ; and what the angry man desires is to take revenge for that slight conspicuously, that is so that his revenge is clearly seen by others. An excellent example of the truth of what Aristotle says may be found in Shakespeare's *Henry V*. You will remember how the Dauphin sends to the young prince, or young king as he now is, a present of tennis-balls, as much as to say, " You are a young man who have spent your life in all sorts of amusements instead of the business of a prince or king, and we are sending you a present of tennis-balls that you may go on with your amusements and not venture upon war." Henry's reply shows how deeply he has felt the insult :

> We are glad the Dauphin is so pleasant with us :
> His present and your pains we thank you for :
> When we have matched our rackets to these balls,
> We will, in France, by God's grace, play a set
> Shall strike his father's crown into the hazard.
> Tell him he hath made a match with such a wrangler
> That all the courts of France will be disturbed . . .
> And tell the pleasant prince this mock of his
> Hath turned his balls to gun-stones ; and his soul
> Shall stand sore-charged for the wasteful vengeance

> That shall fly with them; for many a thousand widows
> Shall this his mock mock out of their dear husbands;
> Mock mothers from their sons, mock castles down;
> And some are yet ungotten and unborn
> That shall have cause to curse the Dauphin's scorn.
>   . . . and tell the Dauphin
> His jest will savour but of shallow wit,
> When thousands weep more than did laugh at it.

But the rhetorician's business may be to allay rather than to excite anger, and Aristotle accordingly has to consider how anger is placated, how calm of mind is to be secured. Our anger, he says, tends to subside if we feel that the slight was unintentional, or has been repented of, or has been done on impulse, not deliberately. Cassius, for example, in Shakespeare's *Julius Cæsar*, is angry with Brutus because of what he deems a slight :

> That you have wronged me doth appear in this:
> You have condemn'd and noted Lucius Pella
> For taking bribes here of the Sardians;
> Wherein my letters, praying on his side,
> Because I knew the man, were slighted of.

But Cassius is appeased as soon as he is convinced that the slight was unintentional. Finally, death is the great allayer. When Mark Antony stands over Brutus's body he forgets the angry insults which they had interchanged before the battle, and pronounces over him a funeral oration : " This was the noblest Roman of them all." I cannot follow Aristotle further in his interesting analyses of the various emotions from the practical point of view of the orator. Cicero, in his *De Oratore*, gives a delightful instance of an orator having to rise when the audience was prejudiced against him, and of the way in which he gradually allayed their anger and persuaded them to take his view of the case to which they had been at first passionately opposed.

Aristotle goes on next to discuss the question of different types of audiences, for, as you will remember, he has said that a speech is composed not only of the orator and his subject but also of the audience which he addresses. Mr Gladstone used to say that the orator gives back in a shower what he gets from his audience as a vapour. One of the reasons why Burke was not successful as a speaker, although he has left behind speeches that are well worth reading, is that he never gave sufficient attention to the audience he was addressing. Lord Thurlow told Croker that Burke never consulted the feelings and prejudices of his audience, that the difference between Fox and Burke during the American controversy was that Fox always spoke to the House and Burke spoke as if he were speaking to himself; which is perhaps why we read Burke now and do not read Fox. It was impossible for Aristotle, of course, to discuss every kind of audience. An orator must rely on experience and intuition to keep him right, but Aristotle does in a rather interesting way describe certain general types of audience, as, for example, an audience consisting of old men or young men or men in the prime of life, or an audience consisting of wealthy men, etc., etc., and all that he has to say is characterised by the delightful sincerity, the absence of hypocrisy, of the Greek scientific mind. Young men, he tells us, are changeful and fickle in their desires, are fond of honour but fonder still of victory, are fonder of victory than of money. The reason for this is that they have never experienced the want of money. They are charitable and they are trustful, as they have not yet been deceived. They are bashful as having yet no independent standard of honour, and have high aspirations for they have not yet been disillusioned by the experience of life. Youth is the age, too, when people are most devoted to their friends. Contrasted with the young, old men are cautious. They "suppose," they never "know," anything, and in discussion they always add "perhaps" or again "possibly." They are uncharitable. They put the worst construction upon everything. They do not trust anybody, from having had experience of human wickedness. They have no strong loves or hatreds. They are cowards and alarmists. They are fond of life, and never so fond of it as on their last day, etc., etc.

It is only the third book of his work that Aristotle devotes to style, but with that I am not now concerned. When with the loss of freedom in Greece and Rome real oratory became, as Milton says, "mute," then rhetoric became very much a study of the refinements and elaborations of artistic prose, figures of speech, and ornament of every kind. The tricks of balance and alliteration which delighted the Elizabethan in the prose of Lyly's *Euphues* go back to Gorgias and the first beginnings of Greek oratory. Cassiodorus, a writer of the sixth century A.D., declares that " It is ornament alone that distinguishes the learned from the unlearned, and, true to this maxim of decadent rhetoric, he obscures the simplest and most trivial statements in a cloud of embellishments " (Bury, *History of the Later Roman Empire* (1923)). But I have gone back to Aristotle and his treatment of rhetoric regarded as the whole art of persuasion just because his treatment is so much larger and so entirely in the spirit of scientific detachment and completeness. For the art of persuasion is very much alive to-day. It may be, as Sir Richard Jebb said, that the best modern oratory is distinguished from that of antiquity by its less deliberate appeal to the feelings, its more intellectual and argumentative character, yet the voice of persuasion and propaganda is loud around us. It cries from every advertisement hoarding. It works in our newspaper press alike by *suggestio falsi* and *suppressio veri*. A great part of literature is a skilful exercise in the art of deceiving that large reading public which the spread of elementary education has made a prey for editors and pub- lishers. The importance of propaganda as a force in democratic countries is seen by the completeness with which all adverse criticism has been suppressed in those countries where freedom has disappeared since the last war. If free speech is the breath of a free people, rhetoric is one of its poisons.

This is rhetoric, then, as Aristotle defines and treats it—the art of persuasion. His work is not, as has been suggested, a treatise on prose-writing corresponding to the short treatise, the *Poetics*. One may use verse to persuade as well as prose. Most of Aristotle's examples are taken from the poets. Of the three books only the last and shortest is devoted to style as such. In our treatment here we shall both enlarge and contract the scope of the study. We shall *enlarge* it, because our remarks will not be confined to oratory, to speech or writing the express aim of which is to persuade, to induce those who hear or read to act in some specific way, if it be merely to subscribe more largely. We shall consider also writing or speaking whose aim is, not to persuade, but merely to convey information, to instruct, to tell us the facts or describe a scene or object of some definite kind. But we shall also endeavour to say something helpful, if not to the creative writer yet to his reader or critic, about composition whose aim, at least its express aim, is neither to instruct nor to persuade, but to give what we call æsthetic pleasure, a work of art, be it poem or prose, romance or essay. On the other hand, our study will be more *confined* than that of Aristotle, because we shall not undertake to deal with the " topics," arguments which the poet or dramatist or novelist may use to effect his purpose of giving imaginative pleasure. For all that Aristotle says of the orator's appeals to the intellect in his proofs, his " topics," and to the emotions, may easily be extended to the work of the poet, the dramatist, the novelist, with certain differences arising from his different aim or purpose. The novelist too, for example, needs proofs to persuade his readers that he is presenting a probable picture of life. Consider, for example, the means by which Defoe has induced readers to accept his picture of what happened in Robinson Crusoe's island, and the way in which Swift has extended Defoe's tricks to the presentation of a to us impossible world. " I do not believe half of it," is said to have been the response of a sea-captain to his reading of *Gulliver's Travels*. Or again, consider the historical novelist. By what means does he, be he Scott or Flaubert, make us willing to believe that things went just thus in past days—the archaic cast of his style, his suggestion of a different moral atmosphere, etc. ? As to the feelings, the emotions, there is nothing which Aristotle says in his analysis of the means of arousing or allaying feeling, this or that particular emotion, which is not used by the poet for his purpose, not of persuading, but of giving imaginative, æsthetic pleasure.

CHAPTER II

THE POINT OF VIEW

For a speech is composed of three things, the speaker, the subject on which he speaks, and the audience he is addressing.—Aristotle : *Rhetoric*, 1. 3.

So Aristotle defines the point of view that must govern the orator's choice of arguments, whether addressed to the intellect or to the emotions, and which must determine the style in which he is to clothe his argument. Different subjects must be handled in different ways ; and not only so, but an argument that is effective in the mouth of one speaker may be quite out of place in the mouth of another speaker. The same applies to the language used ; and finally, what may be an effective argument addressed to an audience of old or rich men will often be quite lost upon an audience of young or poor men, or even incur their active hostility.

Nothing can seem more obvious than this when stated thus generally, and yet there is no greater difficulty for many persons than this, of catching the right note ; nothing which more immediately indicates the born orator than the power to get quickly into touch with his audience. The successful orator is not the great thinker, like Burke. He is the person who puts into words with felicity, and with the appearance of conviction, what his audience already half thinks and wishes to believe. By some innate gift such a speaker divines what his audience wishes him to say. He is not a teacher but an interpreter. He is what the poet is to a wider and yet a more select audience, the utterer of " what oft was thought but ne'er so well expressed." But the orator whose success with popular audiences is overwhelming may fail entirely before a more critical and professional audience. The advocate who can persuade or overawe a jury may not be the best person to employ when the case lies before a bench of judges who demand nothing but a clear statement of the evidence, or a convincing demonstration of the law applicable to the case in dispute. The good platform speaker is not always listened to with the same respect in the House of Commons. What tells with a deliberative body is in the end not so much eloquence as knowledge and wisdom. " Eloquence," Hobbes declared, " is seeming wisdom." The revivalist, again, who moves crowds in California or London may vociferate in vain to the audience that cares only for the still, small voice of the mystic and saint. Of Saint Vincent de Paul the Abbé Huvelin writes : " If one came in quest of genius, such as lived in the eyes of Bossuet, genius which expresses itself in vivid and impetuous sallies, one was a little disappointed. M. Vincent was not of this order. His cast of features is a little heavy, but one loves to listen to him. You are penetrated by the unction of his words. They enter not as an irruption but an infiltration, little by little. It is God himself to whom one is listening."

The point of view, then, determines everything, and not least the speaker's or writer's style, choice of words and images, idiom and order. One has but to turn over the pages of some anthology of English prose to feel almost with every author, certainly with the authors of different periods, the influence of the kind of audience the writer has more or less consciously before him. It is this which explains in great measure the difference between the prose of Dryden and his contemporaries and that of the writers of the preceding age. The great prose writers of the period from Hooker to Milton and Clarendon are, one feels at once, scholars writing for scholars, hence their Latinised vocabulary, their Ciceronian periods, their quotations and allusions—and nothing is more dangerous with an unlearned audience than too many allusions. Macaulay, in many ways a shining example of clear and sparkling writing, yet frequently presupposes a range of knowledge in his reader that is quite beyond even his imaginary schoolboy, far more a popular audience. There had, of course, before the time of Dryden been writers of a simple English prose—Wyclif in the fourteenth century, Latimer in the sixteenth, and Bunyan and others in the seventeenth. But the audience these have in view is obviously simple and unlearned. Bunyan's language is the colloquial English of the day, but he expects that his readers will be familiar with one book, the English Bible. Another type of what one might call popular prose was that of the young pamphleteers, the University wits of the reign of Queen Elizabeth. Their peculiar blend of racy colloquial English with Euphuistic artifice and imagery was intended for an audience of young men about town, men with a tincture of classical learning and a considerable familiarity with contemporary Italian and Italianate literature. It is with Dryden that the audience addressed is, for the first time, an audience at once cultivated and polite but not necessarily learned, an audience of men of the world. Dryden's preference is still for a masculine audience, the critics and wits who frequented Will's coffee-house. Swift had the same predilection, but he preferred to the wits the plain good sense of traders and men of business, the "drapiers" of Dublin and London, the readers for whom Defoe rather than Dryden had catered, plain men liking a plain style. Addison is the first writer who has in his mind the "fair sex," as he always called them. "Let him fine-lady it to the end," Swift says rather contemptuously of Addison. He affects a careless elegance and delicate cadence. It has become more difficult to-day to define the type of audience a writer has in view, for the spread of education has levelled up and down, and complicated the character of the audience a writer may find he has to address. The special knowledge needed to understand a work may be found in people widely divorced from one another in social traditions and prejudices, and these count for more in literature, as in oratory, than understanding. For the practical purposes of a student of rhetoric it may be sufficient to keep in view the difference between a cultivated, and to some extent thoughtful and patient audience, willing to make some effort of attention, and an unlearned, impatient, popular audience which must at all costs be kept amused and interested. The spread of education, the popularity of the picture palace, perhaps of broadcasting, has produced an enormous audience—as publishers are realising—for literary work that makes no demand on the intellect, and authors have learnt more and more of the art of clear and vivid narrative and description. Much in Sir Walter Scott's novels is not tolerated by the general reader to-day.

The relation of the author to his audience has been used by some authors in an interesting way to define the difference between poetry and those forms of composition which may be grouped under the head of oratory, but have much in common with poetry. John Stuart Mill's famous " oratory is heard ; poetry is overheard " is identical with Keble's distinction between oratory which is always, he says, consciously addressed to an audience, and poetry which is the utterance of the poet's feelings when he is, so to say, speaking to himself, giving his feelings the relief of expression without any consciousness of a listener, far less an audience. Cicero, he says, is an orator, Plato a poet, because the former writes as one with a crowded audience before him— " quae agit oratorie agit ; semper sibi fingit theatrum, subsellia, auditores ; instat, urget, effundit omnia quibus animi commoveri possint " ; whereas Plato writes as one indulging himself rather than persuading others—" Plato contra suis in deliciis nunquam non versari videtur : sibi indulgere, non aliis persuadere ; majora ferme significare quam eloqui ; ita pulcherrimis cogitationibus abundare ut plura tamen indicta maneant." Plato would, I think, have been surprised to hear that he wrote for his own pleasure and not to persuade his readers. Again, he compares Burke's famous outcry over Marie Antoinette with Jeremy Taylor's sentence in the funeral sermon on Lady Carberry : the great paragraph in the *Reflections* beginning : " It is now sixteen or seventeen years since I saw the queen of France, then the Dauphiness, at Versailles ; and surely never alighted on this orb, which she hardly seemed to touch, a more delightful vision. I saw her just above the horizon, decorating and cheering the elevated sphere she just began to move in—glittering like the morning star full of life, and splendour, and joy. Oh ! what a revolution ! and what a heart must I have, to contemplate without emotion that elevation and that fall ! Little did I dream when she added titles of veneration to those of enthusiastic, distant, respectful love, that she should ever be obliged to carry the sharp antidote against disgrace concealed in that bosom : little did I dream that I should have lived to see such disasters fallen upon her in a nation of gallant men, in a nation of men of honour and of cavaliers. I thought ten thousand swords must have leapt from their scabbards to avenge even a look that threatened her with insult. But the age of chivalry is gone, etc." " This," says Keble, " if anyone shall call ' above all praise,' if truly magnificent, ' splendid,' I hear and ardently approve ; but if he shall say ' poetically ' I do not quite admit it : for the words in some way seem to me to savour of rhetoric, to be too studiously accommodated to the ears of men. Listen, on the other hand, to the great high-priest of *Living and Dying*, how weightily, in some three words he also describes a lady of rank : ' In all her religion and in all her actions of relation towards God, she had a strange evenness and untroubled passage, sliding towards her ocean of God and of infinity with a certain and silent motion.' Will anyone deny that these words flow from a full heart ? Can anyone doubt that he who spoke so would speak in like manner when sitting silent and alone ? " I confess I doubt it. Taylor's words also betray the artist conscious of the beauty of his words and cadences, but there is a difference. He is not seeking to arouse the feelings of his audience as Burke is. He is seeking to communicate—a very different mood of mind.

For the distinction is interesting but not sound. Nobody speaks or writes to be heard of himself only. " Lonely thinking," says Nietzsche, " that is wise ; lonely singing stupid." The bards who

> died content on pleasant sward
> Leaving great verse unto a little clan   (Keats)

were not content to die unnamed because they had expressed their own emotions, but because they had clothed in the beauty of words and music the emotions and aspirations of their little clan, had made themselves the mouthpiece of a community. The earliest poetry is not individual—what does Homer tell us of himself ?—it is the utterance of a people's heart. And if poetry has grown more and more individual, that does not imply that the poet has grown indifferent to his possible audience, careless of sympathy. No one suffers more than the poet who feels that his song finds no echo in the hearts of others. This is the burthen of Shelley's most musical laments :

> Away, away, from men and towns,
> To the wild wood and the downs—
> To the silent wilderness
> Where the soul need not repress
> Its music, lest it should not find
> An echo in another's mind,
> While the touch of Nature's art
> Harmonises heart to heart.

" Shelley did not expect sympathy and appreciation," says his wife, " from the public ; but the want of it took away a portion of the ardour that ought to have sustained him while writing.

He was thrown on his own resources, and on the inspiration of his soul ; and wrote because his mind overflowed, without the hope of being appreciated."

The difference lies rather in the *kind* of audience that each has in mind, and *what* he wants to achieve. The orator is conscious of addressing a number of people of various kinds. His arguments and style must be such as will appeal to the many, the average man, or the average representative of the kind of audience he is addressing. Moreover, he is more bent on exciting the feelings of his audience than on simply communicating his own emotion. He is a scene-painter more intent on large and striking effects than on the delicate delineation of the feeling that inspires himself. The poet whom Mill and Keble have in view appeals to the individual. He writes for the sympathetic listener, one who, he thinks, will understand and sympathise with his emotion. He is not indifferent to whether he has an audience, but he is so eager for sympathy that his audience must be fit even though few. He does not wish to be *half* understood. His aim is perfect comprehension and sympathy. He will not say more than he feels ; he will not say less. It is for this that he has chosen every word, conscious not only of its general meaning but of the exact shade of colour in which association has dyed it ; for this that he has studied the appropriate melody and rhythm of every phrase. He does not wish to cast pearls before swine. He writes for those who have ears to hear.

But this distinction does not mark off poetry from oratory or prose. It is a distinction which cuts across both. There are preachers who care only for this intimate appeal, who prefer deep to broad effects ; and there is, on the other hand, poetry which is quite legitimately oratorical in cast and appeal. Quite legitimately, I say, because the feelings which the poet is expressing are those which belong to us not as individuals but as members of a community, as what Aristotle calls " political animals." When Swinburne sings

> Ask nothing more of me, sweet ;
>   All I can give you I give.
>   Heart of my heart, were it more,
> More would be laid at your feet :
>   Love that should help you to live,
>   Song that should spur you to soar,

we feel that it is very beautiful, but are a little surprised to learn that it is addressed to Liberty. Certainly, but for the last line, we should have thought it was a love poem. And if we admit that Liberty may be invoked in this intimate, personal way, we must also admit that to stir men's blood a more oratorical and vehement note is likely to have a greater effect :

> Yet, Freedom ! yet thy banner, torn but flying,
> Streams like the thunderstorm *against* the wind ;
> Thy trumpet voice, though broken now and dying,
> The loudest still the tempest leaves behind.   (Byron.)

And both these passages are poetry, for both are what Dante calls " musice composita " ; of the effect of both the metrical form is an essential constituent.

When we turn from the audience as a factor in any composition to the subject-matter, we are faced with equally obvious but equally complex considerations. Every subject has its appropriate style. Not only will a historian write, on the whole, in a different style from a philosopher, but the historian of a simple, primitive people, the chronicler, for example, of what Freeman calls the " scuffles on the downs " of early English tribes, would be guilty of a flagrant absurdity if he affected the majestic rhythms and purple magnificence of Gibbon's *Decline and Fall of the Roman Empire* or the kinematic and dramatic vividness of Carlyle's *French Revolution*. But here again it is impossible to prescribe rules or to forecast what will be the appropriate style. The same subject-matter may be approached from so many different angles that it splits up, so to say, into different subjects, each requiring its own treatment, in which the writer's guide, as with the mind and feelings of his audience, can only be experience and intuition. But as it is useful to distinguish *broadly* between a learned and a popular audience, so in respect to subject-matter we shall insist on one division, which is of the greatest importance, if not always for style (*lexis*) in the narrower sense of the old treatises, for that other division of rhetoric on which the ancients laid stress, viz. disposition, arrangement (*taxis*).

There are three orders of phenomena of which the human mind is always aware, of which it has " knowledge by acquaintance," as of a world outside itself, not at all, or very partially and painfully, affected by the human will : these are (1) the order of phenomena in space, the relative position of co-existing things ; (2) the order of phenomena in time, events following one another ; (3) the order of thoughts in the mind, the logical dependence of one truth upon another, or, it may be, the manner in which one thought tends to evoke another even when there is no logical connection between them. To the last of these corresponds all expository literature, from such a piece of rigid reasoning as a paper on mathematics to a literary essay like that of Hume on Miracles, or the playful demonstration of a paradox. The concern of rhetoric is, of course, not with the validity of the reasoning but with the best manner in which it may be set forth to a special, or more often a quite general audience. The second of these orders is the subject-matter of all writing of a historical character, whether the events be real or fictitious ; and its special difficulty arises from the fact that it is impossible for the human mind to follow the succession of more than a limited number of events. How are we to make clear to a reader a number of coincident events, e.g. the incidents of a complicated battle in the course of which many important events were taking place at the same time, when the writer or speaker can only narrate one sequence at a time ? The first of the orders mentioned above is the field of all descriptive writing, from the accurate description of the plan of a house or field or any similar thing to the imaginative landscape of a poet. The difficulty arises again from the difference between the medium and the subject-matter. Words succeed one another in a single stream : how are we by a medium which thus flows to evoke in the mind of a reader the picture of something whose parts are co-existent ? There are few more difficult problems ; and the wise historian generally supplements his verbal description with maps and plans. The wise imaginative writer eludes the difficulty and, while presenting vivid details, leaves the reader to fit these into a framework of his own composing. Take the first verse of Gray's " Elegy " :

> The curfew tolls the knell of parting day,
> The lowing herd wind slowly o'er the lea,
> The plowman homeward plods his weary way,
> And leaves the world to darkness and to me.

The details here given are sufficient to call up a picture of evening in the mind of every reader, but the picture evoked by one reader will differ in innumerable respects from that of another. Each will supply from his own experience, from particular landscapes that linger in his memory, what the poet has left out.

The effect of the speaker himself on what he says—which Aristotle places first among the three factors—is of course a very real one, but for theoretical discussion somewhat intangible. " Le style, c'est l'homme même." A great writer's style is as individual as his voice and gait. It bears the mark of his whole intellectual and moral constitution. According to Aristotle and the ancient writers on rhetoric, arguments addressed to the mind, even well-calculated appeals to the feelings, are generally less effective than the impression of the speaker's own character, his ability, integrity, and good-will, which he communicates to his listeners ; every other appeal is fortified by this. But what is true of the orator is true of every great writer. His personality attracts or repels us. Nietzsche's thumbnail sketches of certain authors are a record of his irritable dislike of the personality revealed in the style—" Rousseau, or the return to Nature, *in impuris naturalibus*. . . . Dante, or the Hyena that writes poetry on tombs. . . . Victor Hugo, or the Lighthouse on the sea of nonsense. . . . Carlyle, or Pessimism after undigested meals. John Stuart Mill, or offensive lucidity. . . . Zola, or the love of stinking."

But these splenetic definitions are an index to Nietzsche's own character—or his health of mind. For the charm as well as the greatness of the character revealed in the work of writers has found expression in phrase and poem as well as in deliberate critical analysis. The sweetness of Shakespeare's nature, " Fancy's child," was felt and recorded even before the mysterious greatness of his dramatic insight was fully comprehended, and it is still an ingredient in every appreciation :

Thence came the honeyed corner at his lips,
The conquering smile wherein his spirit sails
Calm as the God who the white sea-wave whips,
Yet full of speech and intershifting tales,
Close mirrors of us ; thence had he the laugh
We feel is thine [that is the Earth's], broad as ten thousand beeves
At pasture.   (Meredith.)

Modern criticism has made this interpretation of the personality revealed in a writer's art one of its principal tasks in place of the old testing by rules or recording of beauties and faults; and Charles Lamb was the first, and, despite some capriciousness, is perhaps still the greatest master of such criticism.

But personality and its communication cannot be inculcated by the teacher. There is, however, one element of character which may be abstractly considered in its effect on style, and that is *purpose*. Whatever be the nature of the audience addressed, or the subject-matter—philosophical, historical, descriptive—the manner in which we are to treat the theme will depend also on the purpose we have in view, the motive which has induced us to speak or write. Sir Harry Lauder and the late Mr Spurgeon had both the power of appealing to a popular audience, but they did not do it in the same way, for the purpose of the one was very different from that of the other. The aim of the comedian was to leave his audience contented with themselves and with him, contented and cheerful; the aim of the preacher was to leave his hearers discontented with themselves, disillusioned with regard to this life, and dismayed by the prospect of the next, but with a glimpse of something in attaining to which dismay and disillusionment and discontent would vanish. The most eloquent speaker is not always the most persuasive. The final test of a speech or a sermon is, what does it make us do?—lead a new life? or increase our subscription? A sermon fails if it leaves us merely delighted with its own beauty of eloquence; although, of course, it may be the aim of a sermon not to make us act but to make us willing to suffer, or to elevate and console.

The purposes of men are infinite in number, but for a treatise on Rhetoric we may reduce the motives which induce us to speak or write at any time to three general categories—to convey information, to induce others to act in a certain way, or thirdly, to give pleasure, to interest and delight by wit, feeling, or imagination. These different aims are, of course, like the divisions we have made of audience and subject-matter, not mutually exclusive; some information must be conveyed in every kind of writing, some communication of ideas. Again, it is not often really that we speak or write without wishing to influence, to persuade. This is the primary motive from which all literature has sprung. But on the other hand it is also true that the beauty of the medium may and does become an end in itself. There are many works written with a view to convey information or to persuade to action which are now read for the sake of neither, but for the beauty of the style. It is, however, easy to find examples in which one or other of these three motives is dominant, is the shaping and colouring factor in the writer's style. At one extreme we may have a proposition of Euclid, a mathematical proof (for the language of formulæ is the ideal language in which to convey precise information, abstract, colourless, exact), and at the other extreme a lyrical poem such as " Tears, idle tears," or " O world, O Life, O Time," or " Behold her, single in the field," where the thought counts for little or nothing apart from the colour and music of the images and the words by which it is communicated. Between these extremes lies a whole countryside, field melting into field. The specialist, writing on physiology or numismatics, need think of nothing in regard to style but clearness and precision—qualities how rarely attained ! Everything else is an intrusion, and an unnecessary intrusion, because he can count upon willing and patient readers who desire to study the subject. But every writer is not so fortunate. A lecturer or writer may know that if he is to find people willing to receive the information, the instruction he wishes to convey, he must interest and attract, and precision of statement may have to be sacrificed to the popular taste for definite and easily understood conclusions. Lucidity may be insufficient without the assistance of force of expression or beauty of style. The treatises of Aristotle, as they have come down to us, were obviously prepared solely for students. Tradition tells us that he had a more oratorical style in popular writings. Plato had a wider audience in view. Aristotle is content to instruct, Plato desires to influence. In some fields instruction passes at once into persuasion. In dealing with ethical, religious, and political topics, writers instruct as a rule in order that they may persuade. The head is an avenue to the heart and the will. And if the instructor easily becomes the persuasive orator, the orator passes readily into the region of the poet, the purely imaginative writer whose aim is not action but contemplation. Plato had a practical end in view always—the just state and the just citizen— but he was well aware that the end he sought was an ideal, and when he turns aside to elaborate the myth of the charioteers in the *Phædrus* or the myth of Er in the *Republic* he is not giving information (myths are not history) nor is he directly exhorting ; he is revealing in a vision the intuitions of a prophet and poet.

This threefold distinction between writings that instruct the understanding, those that sway the will, and those that delight the imagination will be found to correspond to, and explain, a good many of the divisions we commonly make in composition and literature. From it springs a division, that was frequent in treatises on rhetoric, of the qualities of style into (1) intellectual—simplicity (a relative conception), clearness or lucidity, and precision ; and (2) emotional qualities, which are divisible just as the emotions themselves are, but broadly comprise two main kinds of effect—beauty, what attracts and delights, and sublimity, or the qualities which overawe even while they too delight us.

The difference, moreover, of purpose provides a more crucial distinction between oratory and poetry, taking poetry for the moment to cover purely imaginative writing. It is the persuasive purpose, the practical intention, the end beyond itself which characterises oratory, whatever form it may take (speech, leading articles, essay, didactic poem, or novel with a purpose), and distinguishes it from literature which has no aim beyond itself, no purpose in view but the pleasure, the æsthetic delight, which it affords to the senses and the imagination. But this " pleasure " includes a great deal. At its lowest or simplest the pleasure may be little more than a gay or pensive mood of feeling evoked by a simple strain of song. Wordsworth complains of those who talk of a taste for poetry " as if it were a thing as indifferent as a taste for rope dancing or Frontiniac or Sherry." Well, it is of the same kind ; and a taste for reading novels and poems of a kind is perhaps quite as common a thing as a discerning palate. Further, a too exclusive concern with form in literature gives to a taste even for the best poetry this hedonistic cast, robs it of a little of the high seriousness which a love of poetry, like all love, should manifest. For the " pleasure " which imaginative literature aims at providing includes something which is not on a lower scale than conduct—which is the concern of the best didactic and oratorical writing—but something to which both philosophy and theology have assigned the highest place of all, namely contemplation, the impassioned vision of the worth of things. Poetry has often taken its rise from a practical purpose, *e.g.* Lucretius's great poem, but its final value as poetry does not depend on any practical effect it may achieve, but on its revelation of emotional truth, of what we call *value*. Oratory, persuasive writing, is a kind of table-land connecting two great peaks that rise into a higher and more untroubled atmosphere, science and poetry— the colourless vision of the world of objects and universals, things in their relation to one another ; and at the other extremity the impassioned but equally true vision and revelation of the value which things have for the human heart. Statements such as

> As flies to wanton boys, are we to the gods,
> They kill us for their sport,

are, in a different sphere, of the same kind as the great generalisations of science, the hypothesis of the atoms, or the kinetic theory of light, electricity, and magnetism. They are not ultimate truths, it may be. But as the theory is the fullest outcome of a great mind's thought regarding the phenomena to be explained, the last revealing word that, at the stage reached, science can utter, so the poem, the great poetic phrase or line, is the sincere and supreme expression of the heart—the heart which is as full of mysteries which only genius can reveal as is the world of nature. Rhetoric, aiming at persuasion, uses both scientific truth and genuine emotion for a practical purpose, and in so doing is apt to alloy both.

CHAPTER III

THE CHOICE OF WORDS

Primoque in libro dixerit (Cæsar) verborum dilectum originem esse eloquentiae.—Cicero : *Brutus*, 72, 253.

WE start, then, from the point of view that there are no rules for composition which are of absolute validity. All are relative to and derived from consideration of the subject we are speaking about, the audience we are addressing, and the end that we have in view. Each of these is capable of infinite subdivision. No rules will take the place of intuition and experience in teaching us to recognise when face to face, actually or in imagination, with a certain audience that only *one* style is suitable, and what that style is, simple or ornate, argumentative or impassioned. For general purposes, however, we have distinguished (1) between a specialist and a popular audience, (2) between expository or argumentative, historical, and descriptive subjects, (3) between an instructive, a persuasive, and a purely æsthetic or imaginative purpose. It is then with a continual reference, explicit or implicit, to these differences in audience, subject, and purpose that we propose to discuss the elements of style, and in the first place the words we use.

The right choice of words, said Cæsar, is the fountain-head of eloquence. To understand this we must realise all that words are to the literary artist. To the philologist (in the narrower sense of the word) words are arbitrary signs, blocks gradually shaped and weathered by the laws which govern change of sound and change of meaning, the laws which are investigated by phonetics and semantics. To the poet and orator they are living things, *epea pteroenta*, the winged messengers of their thoughts and feelings, and like the birds they have three properties—body or meaning, colour, and music. Of these the first—though without it the others would quickly lose their value—is for literary purposes often the least important. It is what the dictionaries attempt to define, the thing, quality, action, relation which the word stands for, which it recalls to the mind of the hearer or reader. A glance at the dictionary will show how vague and manifold this meaning often is ; and the scientific writer, for whom meaning is every-thing, is glad to escape from words of everyday use to symbols which he can define more precisely.

But for the artist in speech words have other qualities on a due regard for which depend the finer effects, which make literature something quite different from a succession of colourless algebraic or chemical formulæ. The first of these I have called " colour " for want of a less metaphorical name. I mean by " colour " the associations which gather around a word by long usage. The meaning provides the first nucleus for this, and then come all the accidental circumstances connected with our experience of the word—the people who used it, the places in which we have heard it, the other words and ideas that it tends to evoke. And so we find that, against or with our will, some words are vulgarised, savour (for we might speak of " taste " as well as " colour ") of the streets and the music-hall ; others are homely, though any-thing but vulgar, are redolent (all the senses claim a share in these associations) of home, of familiar objects and experiences, of the farm-yard, the fishing-boat and the workshop ; others are pedantic, schoolmasters' words that no healthy-minded boy ever uses in the playground—" ink-horn terms," the Elizabethans called them ; and other words are dignified, learned it may be but not pedantic, for a learned word is only pedantic when it takes the place of a simpler and more obvious one ; and some words retain even isolated in the dictionary the sublimity of their original significance —the " sea," the " sun," the " stars," " birth," and " death," and " immortality " ; and again others are lovely exotics that only the poets have ventured to use : " At length burst in the *argent* revelry." How far this " colour " is dependent on the individual word, how far upon its setting, its association with other words, and certain other questions arising out of this distinction between words and words—notably the famous dispute regarding poetic diction—are subjects which shall receive consideration in due course.[1]

---

[1] Burke was one of the first writers on æsthetics to note the emotional value of the colour given to words by associations : " The common notion of the power of poetry and eloquence, as well as that of words in ordinary conversation, is

Words, finally, have not only significance and colour but also melody and rhythm. There are euphonious and there are unpleasing words. The factors which produce these results are probably more complex than we are immediately conscious of. Some of them concern the mouth rather than the ear. They are sympathetic muscular effects. When we listen to a speaker, or when we read, we speak with him, we consciously or unconsciously pronounce the words. Some readers are slow to lose the habit of doing so consciously and audibly. But some words are pleasant to utter, sweet on the tongue and gentle on the lips ; others require an effort, a violent discharge of breath through the throat or lips. Again, rhythm is a muscular effect in which both mouth and ear participate. It is easier to utter and pleasanter to hear an interchange of stressed and unstressed sounds than too long a succession of one or the other. And in some words these effects are combined, the voice rising and falling easily as it passes from one pleasant combination of vowel and consonant to another—" incarnadine," " co-eternal." The old lady who spoke with rapture of the blessed word " Mesopotamia " was doubtless quite incapable of analysing her impressions, but we may conjecture that, if biblical " colour " was an essential factor, the other was the rhythmical succession of consonants and vowels. But ease of pronunciation and rhythm are not the only musical qualities of words and syllables. They have also pitch or tone. In this respect

that they affect the mind by raising in it ideas of those things for which custom has appointed them to stand." Having then classified words, he takes the particular case of what he calls " compound abstracts such as virtue, honour, persuasion, docility. Of these I am convinced, that whatever power they may have on the passions, they do not derive it from any representations raised in the mind of the things for which they stand." [Too elaborate an analysis is required to obtain distinct conceptions.] " Such words are in reality but mere sounds ; but they are sounds which being used on particular occasions, wherein we receive some good, or suffer some evil ; or see others affected with good or evil; or which we hear applied to other interesting things or events ; and being applied in such a variety of cases that we know already by habit to what things they belong, they produce in the mind, whenever they are afterwards mentioned, effects similar to those of their occasions. The sounds being often used without reference to any particular occasion, and carrying still their first impressions, they at last utterly lose their connexion with the particular occasions that give rise to them ; yet the sound, without any annexed notion, continues to operate as before."—Burke : *On the Sublime and Beautiful*, v. 2.

languages differ very much from one another. The Greek accent was a pitch-accent. In certain dialects pitch is very marked. Investigation shows, however, that it is an element in every language and constitutes one of the subtler factors with which, as with alliteration — the pleasing juxtaposition of vowel and consonant sounds—the poet produces his finer effects.[1]

Rules for the use of words are thus bound to be of a very relative character, relative to our first three heads, subject, audience, purpose, and also to other things in a word than its meaning alone. Take, to begin with, the two principles on which the old rhetoricians laid great stress—purity and propriety : the use of good English words in their proper significance, the meaning which usage has assigned to them. " Let all our words," says Quintilian, " and even our tone of voice, if possible, declare

---

[1] Euphony, as we may call all these factors of rhythm, melody, and easy pronunciation, is an element in which different languages vary more than is possible in any other respect. Most modern languages are rich enough in words, though in certain fields one may be able to express more varied shades of meaning than another. In every language words acquire colour from association, multiplex shades of feeling that only a native can appreciate. Association doubtless makes even the sound of one's native language sweet to the ear. But no association will ever disguise the fact that Italian is a more euphonious language than guttural Dutch or German with its spluttering sch—s—ts (z) sounds. What English has gained from the absorption of classical polysyllables rich in labials and open vowels, the student of Shakespeare and Milton can judge :

> The multitudinous seas incarnadine.

> Then feed on thoughts that voluntary move
> Harmonious numbers.

Doubtless the gain has its countervailing perils. Thomson and Cowper with their " irriguous vales " and " stercoracious heaps " (to say nothing of Dr Johnson) are sufficient proof. English poetry had to invigorate itself at the end of the eighteenth century by re-entering the stream of native and colloquial, including dialectal, speech ; but it was able to do so without sacrificing what the usage of great writers had consecrated. It is by the blend of native and classical elements that English writers have achieved their greatest effects of colour and harmony, have blended strength with euphony.

" In the facility and force of compound epithets the German from the number of its cases and inflections approaches to the Greek, that language so

> Bless'd in the marriage of sweet words.

It is in the woeful harshness of its sounds alone that the German need shrink from the comparison."—Coleridge : *Biographia Literaria.*

us to be natives of this city, that our speech may appear truly Roman, and not merely to have been admitted into citizenship." The justification of such a rule needs no elaboration. Whether we wish to be understood or to please or to move (" docere vel delectare vel permovere "), we are likely to succeed best if the words and the idioms which we use are at once intelligible to our hearers and endeared to them by long association. The charm of some authors is found in the genuinely English flavour alike of their vocabulary and their idiom. The difficulty begins when we attempt to define " good English " and to rule out certain classes of words. Campbell defines " good " as equivalent to *reputable* (used by authors of good repute—a little of a circle this, but one that is inevitable : good actions are those which good men do), *national* (*i.e.* neither foreign nor provincial nor technical nor coined for the occasion), and *present* (*i.e.* not archaic, obsolete words). The definition will serve as a rough working rule, but it has one omission of importance, and it may be used in a positively misleading fashion. Campbell overlooks—and this is characteristic of the period of Johnsonese prose—a distinction on which modern grammarians lay great stress, namely that between the spoken and the written language. In guarding against vulgarisms and slang he forgets that it is almost as undesirable to speak like a book, and what applies to the spoken tongue is true of writing, *e.g.* letter-writing, whose charm consists in the preservation of the spoken tone. It is a fault that half-educated people are liable to, the use in conversation and informal communications of stilted, pedantic expressions.[1]

---

[1] Dr Johnson's conversation could be racy enough, yet he often spoke not only like a book but like a lexicographer, and when he wrote he translated the colloquial into the Johnsonian. But even Johnsonese in Johnson's mouth is vigorous, precise, and weighty. It was in his imitators, especially ladies, that the Johnsonian style became intolerable. There is probably no worse prose in English than that of the Johnsonian tradition—for which Johnson was not alone responsible—with its conventional dressing of simple statements in literary attire. Compare the racy colloquial style of *Evelina* with that of Miss Burney's later novels. Look at Mrs Radcliffe's style, which has its qualities but runs too much in this vein : " In the solitude of his confinement the Marquis de Montelt had leisure to reflect on the past and to repent of his crimes ; but reflection and repentance formed as yet no part of his disposition. He turned with impatience from recollection which produced only pain, and looked forward to the future with an endeavour to avert the disgrace and punishment which

But more important than this omission is the fact that there is no one of the classes which Campbell's definition tends to rule out that will not on occasion supply the very word which ought to be used. " Good English " is not a definite or definable collection of words; what is the right word depends on the subject one is speaking about and the audience one is speaking to. Technical terms, for example, were forbidden in general use by some of the older writers on Rhetoric, and Lindley Murray in his *English Grammar, Adapted to the Different Classes of Learners* (1798), gives this delightful example of the application of the rule. " Most of our hands," he quotes from some book of travels, " were asleep in their berths when the vessel shipped a sea that carried away our pinnace and binnacle. Our deadlights were in or we should have filled. The mainmast was so sprung that we were obliged to fish it, and bear away for Lisbon." This he then recasts as follows : " Most of our sailors were asleep in their apartments, when a heavy wave broke over the ship and swept away one of our boats, and the box which contained our compasses, etc. Our cabin windows were secured or the vessel would have been filled. The mainmast was so damaged that we were obliged to strengthen it, and to proceed for Lisbon." The meaning *may* be there, but what has become of the colour ? The " race " of the original has been watered down to the conventional elegance of " young ladies' " academies like that of the Misses Pinkerton where Johnson's dictionary and Johnson's *Rambler* were the final authorities on vocabulary and style. Technical terms are the very juice of many passages of excellent prose and verse, exact and concrete in meaning, rich in associations. Shakespeare has all the technical

---

he saw impending. The elegance of his manners had so effectually veiled the depravity of his heart, that he was a favourite with his sovereign ; and on this circumstance he rested his hope of security." This is the style of *The Rambler* and *Rasselas* applied to romantic fiction ; and even Sir Walter Scott when not reproducing racy dialect or painting a picture in the style of Teniers, is content to lapse into a careless version of this tawdry literary dressing : " Here like one of those lovely forms which decorate the Landscapes of Poussin Waverley found Flora gazing on the waterfall. . . . The sun now stooping in the west gave a rich and varied tinge to all the objects which surrounded Waverley, and seemed to add more than human brilliancy to the full expressive darkness of Flora's eye, exalted the richness and purity of her complexion, and enhanced the dignity and grace of her beautiful form," etc., etc.

terms of hawking, hunting and coursing at his finger-ends, and some of his thrilling phrases are metaphorical applications :

> Not one of them
> Dares stir a wing if Warwick shake his bells.

> If I do prove her haggard,
> Though that her jesses were my dear heart-strings,
> I'd whistle her off, and let her down the wind
> To prey at fortune.

And what is true of technical is true, in their proper place, of dialectal, foreign, archaic and colloquial words. The novel of country and local life has given a place in literature to the dialects that exist, and for long will exist, beside the standard language. The historical novel has found that its due colour could only be preserved by a certain archaism of language, though the exact amount required depends on circumstances.[1] Similarly stories or descriptions of foreign, e.g. Indian life, would fail of their effect without an admixture of strange names for strange things, and even when our knowledge of the thing itself remains vague the words breathe of enchantment and create an atmosphere. And as regards colloquial, even slang words, not only the novelists but the poets have shown that Wordsworth's denial of any difference between the language of verse and that of prose is well justified if it be taken to mean no more than this, that it is impossible to prepare a dictionary of words which a poet may

---

[1] Scott, after his experience in editing Strutt's *Queenhoo Hall*, came to the conclusion that to produce the right atmosphere it was sufficient in all cases to go back to the language of our grandfathers. To do more than that is to risk becoming unintelligible. Again it depends on circumstances. It would not do to make the characters in *Ivanhoe* speak Middle-English and Norman-French, any more than in a novel of foreign life to make more than an occasional use of foreign words. It may be doubted whether a novel written in accurate Elizabethan English would be understood and enjoyed. There is a great deal in Shakespeare's language that an untrained Englishman no longer understands. But there are long periods in which the language has changed more slowly. Thackeray's *Henry Esmond* is probably the most brilliant reproduction of the style of a past day. Of course the dialect of the provincial novelist is often as far from being accurate as the " tushery " of the historical novelist. In each case the author is safe to presume on the ignorance of his audience. It is enough if Sir James Barrie's Scotch, Mr Kipling's Irish and Yorkshire, have sufficient resemblance to what most people think is Scotch, Irish or Yorkshire. Art, as Plato complained, is concerned with appearances, not realities.

use and another of words which he must leave alone.[1] Finally,
even if we set aside special kinds, like the historical or provincial
novel, it will be found that whenever style begins to require colour
the writer begins to use words which Campbell's definition would
exclude, and literary as opposed to scientific writing begins when
style becomes coloured and rhythmical.

The same relativity attaches to the rule of propriety. It is
easy to lay down that words must not be used in a sense which
they do not bear, that " Herculanean " must not be used when
we mean " Herculean," that " avocation " is not the same thing
as " vocation," nor " eliminate " as " elicit," nor " transpire "
as " happen." But this carries us a very little way. The English
language is perhaps peculiarly exposed to this kind of error
because of the large number of foreign, especially Latin and
Greek, roots used in forming new words. In a language which,
like German, makes its compounds out of native words, it is
easier to understand the compound made from these words and to
control misapplication. A large number of the examples which
Hodgson quotes in his *Errors in English* of words of classical
origin misused are taken from works by women, with whom a
classical education was the exception ; and our newspapers
abound in similar errors. It may indeed be questioned whether
after a time it does not become pedantic to contend against
certain misuses as against certain mispronunciations. Some words

---

[1] Coleridge, who criticised Wordsworth—I have given above what I take
to be the keystone of his position—recognises quite clearly that a specifically
poetic vocabulary is an accident of languages at a certain stage of their
development. " Where there are a few literary men and the vast $\frac{9,999,999}{10,000,000}$
of the population are ignorant, as was the case of Italy from Dante to Metastasio,
from causes I need not here put down, there will be a poetical language :
[One might instance also the vocabulary of the Homeric poems, of the early
Norse court poetry and of Anglo-Saxon poetry] but that a poet ever uses a word
as poetical—that is formally—which he, in the same mood and thought, would
not use in prose or conversation, Milton's prose works will assist us in dis-
proving. But as soon as literature becomes common and critics numerous in any
country, and a large body of men seek to express themselves habitually in the
most precise, sensuous and impassioned words the difference as to mere words
ceases. . . . The sole difference in style is that poetry demands a severe keeping
—it admits nothing that prose may not often admit but it oftener rejects. In other
words it presupposes a more continuous state of passion." *Anima Poetæ.*

in English owe their present meaning to mistaken etymologies, and we can occasionally see the process going on before our eyes. A good example is the verb " demean." The root-sense is preserved in the noun " demeanour," and we still use the verb correctly when we speak of a person " demeaning himself ill or well." But a mistaken connection with " mean " is establishing the use of the word in the sense of " lower "—" I will not demean myself by replying to such a charge " we have heard from so good a writer as Lord Bryce. The fact is that the word to a certain extent supplies a want. " I will not lower myself " would do, but the general use of " lower " in the quite literal sense (" He lowered himself from the window ") has prevented its acquiring colour, and it is not only meaning but colour which " demean " has absorbed from the adjective " mean." " Avocation " in like manner has come to be used for " daily occupation," [1] because the etymology has been forgotten and because the more correct " vocation " has a rather stronger meaning, not merely " profession " or " occupation," but that to which a man feels himself specially called or devoted. A clergyman likes to speak of his profession as a " vocation," and so do most people who make a business of improving others.

It is the fact that words have colour and euphony as well as significance that justifies or comes near to justifying Professor Raleigh's statement, " Let the truth be said outright : there are no synonyms, and the same statement can never be repeated in a changed form of words."

In the first place, colour and significance as definable by the dictionary are mutually at work on one another. The meaning is the first root of the associations which give colour, but as these associations multiply they give rise to definable distinctions of

---

[1] Gibbon uses the word accurately when he says of Basil : " The ten or twelve years of his monastic life were disturbed by long and frequent avocations " (*Decline and Fall*, ch. 37). " Heaven is his vocation," says Fuller, " and therefore he counts earthly employments avocations." But the O.E.D. recognises that it is commonly used for " ordinary employment, usual occupation, vocation, calling." I have suggested an explanation. One is willing to call one's usual occupation an " avocation," for the word has lost all colour ; one is shy of calling it a " vocation." To say " My vocation is teaching " suggests that one is specially good at it. The effect of English *mauvaise honte* on the language might be worth study.

meaning. "Human" and "humane" are the same word originally, but the latter acquired a colour which has given it at last distinct significance that can be defined—"human" indicating whatever belongs to or is characteristic of man ("To err is human, to forgive divine"), while "humane" is defined as "sympathetic with and considerate for the sufferings of others." But there are many other synonyms which have not yet reached this stage and yet have diverged so far in significance that the one cannot be used in place of the other. The difference is sometimes one of degree, e.g. "ruth" and "pity," of which Professor Raleigh says: "ruth is a quality as much more instinctive and elemental than pity as pitilessness is keener, harder, and more deliberate than the inborn savagery of ruthlessness." Men whose passions have been let loose are for the time being ruthless, like the tempest and the sea. Prussian policy in war is pitiless, deliberately conceived so as to exclude regard for humanity if such regard in any way interferes with its designs. Again, the difference will sometimes be one of degree with at the same time a reference to distinct parts of one general field. "Sympathy" is wider in range than "compassion," and for that very reason dyed in a less warm hue, and "commiseration" has a shade of condescension and contempt that is absent from "compassion." The dictionary that undertook to define these shades of significance would venture on a difficult and hazardous task, for they are elusive and frequently in course of change. But whoever would write well must know and feel them. To the reader of taste there is more offence given by the average journalist's neglect of these finer shades of meaning than by the grosser misusages which one can correct and pass on.

But even when there is no definable or even perceptible difference of meaning between two words there may be an all-important difference of colour. The one word may be erudite, the other homely; the one may be dignified by noble usage, the other vulgarised beyond redemption. It has been said that a grocer and a journalist always "commence," a gentleman is content to "begin." [1] "When Canning wrote the inscription graven on

---

[1] The word "commence" occurs a few times in Shakespeare. It is unknown to the vocabulary of Milton and Shelley. Wordsworth and Tennyson have each used the word twice.

Pitt's monument in the London Guildhall an Alderman felt much disgust at the grand phrase ' he died poor,' and wished to substitute ' he expired in indigent circumstances.' " [1] Dr Jespersen (one of the greatest living authorities on the English language) has discussed the gains and losses to English from the accumulation of synonyms drawn from different but especially classical sources. He has ignored what seems to me one important consideration. It is not merely the pompousness of professors which leads them sometimes to use a coinage from Latin or Greek where a good enough English word already exists. It is due to the desire for definiteness and colourlessness. Everyday words tend to become vague in meaning and rich in association. The scientific writer wishes a word that he can define exactly and that has no irrelevant associations. Even a compound made from native roots is apt to carry with it the colour of the constituent elements. " Insomnia " is less painfully vivid than " sleeplessness," and " cadaver " has not all the emotional associations of " corpse." The use of scientific terms is an approximation to the mathematician's use of colourless formulæ.

Dr Johnson, vigorous and at times homely in conversation, would have excluded from poetry and even from formal prose literature all words that seemed to lack dignity and elegance, and Addison, in some respects his master, had already forbidden to the poet all words " contaminated by passing through the mouth of the vulgar." Johnson maintains that Shakespeare had spoiled a tragic speech by speaking of the " blanket of the dark "— a phrase for stable-boys ! Shakespeare knew that associations fatal to mere dignity and elegance may become potent and penetrating factors in the transfiguring language of passion.

Finally, meaning and colour are not the only considerations in the finding of the *mot propre* : there is also euphony. This it is which forbids—except for special effects—the repetition of the same word at too short an interval, and explains the use of synonyms in : " The Bushman story is just the *sort* of *story* we *expect* from Bushmen, whereas the Hesiodic story is not at all the *kind* of *tale* we *look for* from Greeks " (Lang, *Custom and Myth*, quoted by Jespersen, *op. cit.*). But further, all the factors of euphony

[1] Quoted by Jespersen, *Growth and Structure of the English Language* (19. 2), from Kington Oliphant's *The New English*.

already referred to—balance, rhythm, ease of pronunciation, pitch—will influence a writer in preferring one of several synonyms before the others, and always in so doing he will be asking himself, " How far am I to sacrifice simplicity of meaning (it may be) or the colour of the whole passage to melody and rhythm,[1] or rather how far is my rhythm that which the meaning and colour call for or permit ? "

For the real determining principle in respect of purity and propriety is the harmony of the whole composition as determined by subject, audience, and purpose. That is the principle governing Coleridge's reply to Wordsworth's dictum that there is no essential difference between the language of prose and poetry. The metre constitutes a difference, and a difference which carries others with it, if the harmony of the whole is not to be disturbed.[2] The mood of mind which metre begets and sustains demands also its appropriate diction. There are as many kinds of style as there are speakers and subjects. Still, we can distinguish some main

---

[1] In universum, si sit necesse duram potius atque asperam compositionem malim esse, quam effeminatam ac enervem, qualis apud multos. Ideoque, vincta quaedam de industria sunt solvenda, ne laborata videantur : neque ullum idoneum aut aptum verbum praetermittamus gratia lenitatis.—Quintilian : *Inst.* ix. 4.

[2] " As the elements of metre owe their existence to a state of increased excitement, so the metre itself should be accompanied by the natural language of excitement. . . . As far as metre acts in and for itself, it tends to increase the vivacity and susceptibility both of the general feelings and of the attention. This effect it produces by the continued excitement of surprise, and by the quick reciprocations of curiosity still gratified and still re-excited, which are too slight indeed to be at any one moment objects of distinct consciousness, yet become considerable in their aggregate influence. . . . When therefore correspondent food and appropriate matter are not provided for the attention and feelings thus roused, there must needs be a disappointment felt ; like that of leaping in the dark from the last step of a staircase when we had prepared a leap of three or four. . . . I write in metre because I am about to use a language different from that of prose."—*Biographia Literaria.*

The last statement is somewhat strong. The language of poetry, and good poetry, will frequently differ in no essential respect from that of prose, but it is equally true that if poetry becomes colloquial and prosaic in cast the metre will undergo a corresponding change, or the result is such a jarring lack of harmony as Coleridge describes.

I have quoted in an earlier note a qualification of this earlier view from a later dictum of Coleridge. It does not contradict the principle he lays down here.

D

types, and if the distinction be kept in view it will clear up some of the difficulties as to both purity and propriety.

Cicero, in a passage to which I have referred in an earlier note, distinguishes three main varieties of style—that which is plain, precise and lucid, that which delights by its sweetness and grace, and that which is moving and sublime. I think it would greatly help to clarify certain points to make a fourfold division rather, and to distinguish in the first place a style which might be called no style—the colourless style of the scientific writer. Some of the rules of later rhetoricians apply much more to this style than to any other.

Take, then, a passage from an admirably written history of science in the nineteenth century :

" The train of thought methodically and comprehensively followed out in Gibb's various memoirs had its origin in the early speculations of William Thomson and Clausius, to which I referred above. Thomson was the first who, in adopting (after much hesitation) the mechanical view of the phenomena of heat, the doctrine of the convertibility and equivalence of the different forms of energy, recognised that, in order to describe natural phenomena correctly, this view required a qualification. The change of the different forms of energy into each other can for the most part take place only in one direction ; there is a general tendency in nature towards a degradation or dissipation of energy. Energy, though not lost, becomes less useful, less available. The least available form of energy is heat : and it is in that form that in all natural changes a portion of energy becomes lost, dissipated, or hidden away. Thus we have to recognise the difference between available and unavailable, between useful and useless, energy. In the sequel Thomson showed in definite instances how to calculate the available and the unavailable energy : he introduced the word ' motivity,' the conception of a quantity of a ' possession the waste of which is called dissipation.' Whilst Thomson was thus putting into scientific language and calculating an important and obvious property of nature—namely this, that her processes mainly proceed in a certain definable direction—Rankine and Clausius were labouring independently at the mathematical wording, the analytical expression, of this remarkable discovery. Wherever a change in a system of various elements, factors, or quantities takes place mainly in a definite direction, it is presumable that there exists a definite quantity which is always growing or always decreasing. This quantity may not be directly observable or measurable, as in mechanical motion velocity or distance is directly measurable ; it may be hidden—we may have no special sense with which we can perceive it, as we possess a pressure sense, a heat sense, a sound and light sense ; nevertheless it may be indirectly discoverable, being made up (a function) of definite observable quantities and factors (such as heat, temperature, mass, volume, pressure, etc.) Now Rankine and Clausius found that in all thermal changes or heat processes—and this practically means in all natural processes—there is such a quantity which is always on the increase, and which thus measures in mathematical language the growing loss of available or useful energy in the world. Rankine simply calls it the ' thermo-dynamic function ' ; Clausius thought it important to give it a name which would co-ordinate it with energy, and he called it entropy : energy which is turned inside, become hidden or locked up. Clausius thus gave a different wording of Thomson's doctrine of the universal tendency in nature towards a dissipation of energy by saying, ' The entropy of the world is always on the increase.' " (J. T. Merz, *A History of European Thought in the Nineteenth Century*.)

This comprehensive and well-ordered passage will bear examination from more than one point of view, and we shall recur to it. Meantime it is sufficient to note the character of the diction, and this may be described in two words—precision and colourlessness. The writer has but one end in view, to make his statement of the doctrine in question as lucid as is compatible with accuracy, precision. Note the repetitions made with the purpose of procuring precision—" degradation or dissipation " ; " less useful, less available " ; " lost, dissipated, or hidden away " ; " the mathematical wording, the analytical expression " ; " elements, factors, or quantities " ; " being made up (a function) " ; " hidden or locked up." With this end in view he has no place for irrelevant and distracting colour. The style is the handmaid of the matter— she must not attract attention to herself. A racy homeliness, a decorative elegance or dignity would be equally out of place, and there is no room for passion—and equally intrusive would be the suspicion of rhythm that went beyond the well-balanced placing of clauses co-ordinate or antithetic, and that as unobtrusively as possible.

This style is one which it is in the power of everyone to acquire in some measure, for it is not of course confined to scientific treatises. It is the style in which the modern historian endeavours to write. One wishes he were more often successful in achieving the same lucidity. It is the proper style for a report—the description of a locality, the narration of an incident, a financial statement —whose aim is accuracy. What it demands is a precise use of words, the selecting of the most accurate and colourless words, attention to the logical or psychological laws of clear exposition, as for example (which is often forgotten) that you shall not assume at any stage a knowledge on the part of your audience which they do not yet possess, and finally, adherence to English idiom and the most natural and direct order of words.

The merit of such a style is from another point of view its defect, that it is not literature at all. There is nothing, and intentionally nothing, in the style itself to delight a reader. The work belongs to the " Literature of knowledge," not the " Literature of power." It is more closely akin to a series of mathematical formulæ than to a piece of imaginative literature. Can we indicate any of the more general qualities which at once mark off a piece of writing that we pronounce literary from such exposition as the passage given above ?

In the first place, literature is always more *concrete*. Whether by a more detailed, yet selective, treatment of a concrete subject, or by the use in discussing an abstract subject of concrete illustration, literature always endeavours to remain in closer touch with the concrete world of particular persons and things and places and times. The artist has no desire to follow the scientific writer into this world of colourless universals, or if he does so it is to bring them into touch with the world of our everyday experiences, to show how they do or might modify these. For the politician the discovery of a new force in nature becomes of importance when he can tax it ; to the poet and artist when it brings changes into the world of nature and the relation of man to man.

Again, a work to which we would give the name of literature is generally not only more concrete in its treatment of a subject but also more *decorative*. The word is not a perfect indication of all that is covered by the quality I have in view, but it will suffice and the meaning will become clearer. Dr Merz in the paragraph quoted is anxious only to convey his meaning. It is not his business to make the subject attractive by literary adornment. But in 99 out of 100 of the writings we call literature that is clearly the author's intention. He counts for effect not on the subject-matter alone but on the art not only with which he presents it, but with which he decorates—frills and puffs and pomades. From the leading article with all its stock devices, conventional periphrases, stock metaphors, allusions and quotations, to the beauty of Keats's *Eve of St Agnes* or of Sir Thomas Browne's *Hydriotaphia* or De Quincey's *Suspiria* or Pater's *Leonardo da Vinci*, the literary artist reveals himself as the master of the great craft of cookery—the comparison is as old as Plato—the power of presenting a subject which may or may not have intrinsic worth or interest (the good cook will do wonders with very little, yet good meat is better than bad) with so much charm of diction and figure and rhythm that the imagination is taken captive and one may even be led to believe that Sir Thomas Browne is a thinker like Plato.

Finally, literature is not only more concrete than scientific exposition, and more varied and decorative in the treatment of its theme, it is also, and this is the most fundamental distinction, more *transfiguring*. The aim of the scientific writer, whatever be his subject, is to present it *objectively*, allowing his own feelings to intrude as little as possible, showing things as they are and not as he would have them to be. But the poet, taking him as the highest type of the literary artist, is more concerned not with things as they are in themselves but as they appeal to the imagination and the heart ; and the explanation of a great deal in his diction (as we shall see) is neither vivid portrayal of the concrete for its own sake, nor yet decoration for the sake of decoration, but the subtle and transfiguring portrayal of things seen through the refracting medium of a heated imagination.

These qualities of writing that we call literary are not entirely distinct from one another—as we shall see when we have become more fully intimate with the details in diction and structure of each—still less is any one of them proper to any one style of writing. They are blended in various degrees in all good writing. But nevertheless we may distinguish broadly three main types of style according as one or other of these qualities is dominant; and the question of purity and propriety in the use of words will be seen to resolve itself into this, which of these styles is suitable to the subject and the audience with which I have to deal. It is not a question, often, is this or that word allowable or appropriate? but is the style which the use of such a word suits the suitable style for me just now? Is it not too literary for a familiar letter, or too familiar for a formal address, or too impassioned to express what I really feel? Of course, our style may change in the course of a single speech or essay. Beginning in one key, you may as your audience, real or imaginary, quickens to your touch raise the plane of your address, or lower it. But the vital question is: in the style you wish to adopt is the diction you are using proper to that style?

The threefold division I would make—the colourless, scientific style being a fourth—is into the plain style, the decorative style, and the grand style. I take the last two terms from Sir Joshua Reynolds' division of styles in painting, but they correspond to Cicero's distinction between the style which aims at charming and delighting (*delectare*), and that which aims at moving, seeks to sweep an audience away (*permovere*)—the " sublimity " of Longinus's treatise, whose effect is " not persuasion but transport."

Of the plain style an admirable description has been given by Bishop South (1634-1716), whose sermons are a model of what he commends : " A second property of the ability of speech, conferred by Christ upon his apostles, was its unaffected plainness and simplicity : it was to be easy, obvious and familiar ; with nothing in it strained or far-fetched : no affected scheme, or airy fancies, above the reach or relish of an ordinary apprehension ; no, nothing of all this ; but their grand subject was truth, and consequently above all these petit arts, and poor additions ; as not being capable of any greater lustre or advantage than to appear just as it is. For there is a certain majesty in plainness ; as the proclamation of a prince never frisks it in tropes or fine conceits, in numerous and well-turned periods, but commands in sober, natural expressions. A substantial beauty, as it comes out of the hands of nature, needs neither paint nor patch ; things never made to adorn, but to cover something that would be hid. It is with expression, and the clothing of a man's conceptions, as with the clothing of a man's body. All dress and ornament supposes imperfection, as designed only to supply the body with something from without, which it wanted, but had not of its own. Gaudery is a pitiful and mean thing, not extending farther than the surface of the body ; nor is the highest gallantry considerable to any but to those who would hardly be considered without it : for in that case indeed there may be great need of an outside, when there is little or nothing within.

" And thus also it is with the most necessary and important truths ; to adorn and clothe them is to cover them, and that to obscure them. The eternal salvation and damnation of souls are not things to be treated of with jests and witticisms. And he who thinks to furnish himself out of plays and romances with language for the pulpit, shows himself much fitter to act a part in the revels, than for a cure of souls.

" ' I speak the words of soberness,' said Saint Paul (Acts xxvi, 25) ; and I preach the gospel not with the ' enticing words of man's wisdom ' (1 Cor. ii, 4). This was the way of the apostles' discoursing of things sacred. Nothing here ' of the fringes of the north star ' ; nothing of ' nature's becoming unnatural ' ; nothing of the ' down of angels' wings,' or ' the beautiful locks of cherubims ' ; no starched similitudes introduced with a ' Thus have I seen a cloud rolling in its airy mansion,' and the like. No, these were sublimities above the rise of the apostolic spirit. For the apostles, poor mortals, were content to take lower steps, and to tell the world in plain terms, ' that he who believed should be saved, and that he who believed not should be damned.' And this was the dialect which pierced the conscience, and made the hearers cry out, ' Men and brethren, what shall we do ? ' It tickled not the ear, but sunk into the heart : and when men came from such sermons, they never commended the preacher for his taking voice or gesture ; for the fineness of such a simile, or the quaintness of such a sentence ; but they spoke like men conquered with the overpowering force and evidence of the most concerning truths ; much in the words of the two disciples going to Emmaus : ' Did not our hearts burn within us, while he opened to us the Scriptures ? '

" In a word, the apostles' preaching was therefore mighty, and successful, because plain, natural, and familiar, and by no means above the capacity of their hearers ; nothing being more preposterous than for those who were professedly aiming at men's hearts to miss the mark, by shooting over their heads." (South, *A Sermon preached on the 30th of April* 1668.)

The difference between this and the former passage is obvious. South is as anxious as Merz to make his meaning clear, and it is the meaning he is concerned with, the truth he wishes to drive home. He is not, he expressly disclaims being, anxious to clothe or adorn it in any way. But the thought is a much simpler one than Dr Merz's description of a complex development in scientific theory. All that South has to say could be put into a sentence or two. But that thought is not theoretical like Dr Merz's, but practical. It is an exhortation addressed to the will. The preacher has to combat prejudice, to discredit another view of good preaching—Jeremy Taylor's. It is not enough to say a thing once, he must reiterate, hammer it in ; and it is not enough that the style be lucid, colourless and cold, it must have heat and the colour that heat gives. And so it acquires literary quality, and that quality is a striking plainness, an effective absence of decoration. The words are simple, though not so much so as to imply the presence of an uneducated audience, rather suggesting an auditory of business men, men accustomed to come bluntly to the point, the middle class to which Defoe and Swift appealed. The diction and phrasing are colloquial. The images are drawn from the experience of every day. The sentences tend to be short ; the order of the words natural and direct. This is one variety of literary style and one by which very great effects can be achieved. Latimer, Bunyan, Defoe, Swift, Cowper in his letters, Southey, Cobbett—are some of the masters of the plain style in English prose, and in our day the style of the best journalism has been redeemed from conventional and tawdry ornament by the nervous and supple prose of writers like Mr Belloc and Mr Chesterton. If the plain style is akin to the colourless by its strict attention to the thought, the meaning—a close relevance to which is its highest quality—on the other hand the plain style is capable of becoming the finest thread in the texture of the grand style.

The proper contrast to the plain style is not the grand but the decorative, the ornate style ; and South points the contrast by his references to Jeremy Taylor, one of the most elaborately ornate of English preachers and prose-writers. What Keble admires and South deprecates, not without a touch of contempt, may be illustrated by the same paragraph : " In all her religion, and all her actions of relation towards God, she had a strange evenness and untroubled passage, sliding towards her ocean of God and of infinity with a certain and silent motion. So have I seen a river deep and smooth passing with a still foot and a sober face, and paying to the *fiscus*, the great exchequer of the sea, the prince of all the watery bodies, a tribute large and full : and hard by it a little brook skipping and making a noise upon its unequal and neighbour bottom : and after all its talking and bragged motion, it payed to its common audit no more than the revenues of a little cloud, or a contemptible vessel. So have I sometimes compared the issues of her religion to the solemnities and famed outsides of another's piety ; it dwelt upon her spirit, and was incorporated with the periodical work of every day ; she did not believe that religion was intended to minister to fame and reputation, but to pardon of sins, to the pleasure of God, and the salvation of souls. For religion is like the breath of heaven ; if it goes abroad into the open it scatters and dissolves like camphire : but if it enters into a secret hollowness, into a close conveyance, it is strong and mighty, and comes forth with vigour and great effect at the other end, at the other side of this life, in the days of death and judgment."

There is a flavour of older fashions in the decorative beauty of such a passage, but set beside it a paragraph from a modern author (and in the case of neither am I taking extreme instances), and the same impression is gathered : " As I thus lay, between content and longing, a faint noise stole towards me through the pines. I thought, at first, it was the crowing of cocks or the barking of dogs at some very distant farm ; but steadily and gradually it took articulate shape in my ears, until I became aware that a passenger was going by upon the high-road in the valley, and singing loudly as he went. There was more of good-will than grace in his performance ; but he trolled with ample lungs ; and the sound of his voice took hold upon the hillside and set the air shaking in the leafy glens. I have heard people passing by night in sleeping cities ; some of them sang ; one, I remember, played loudly on the bagpipes. I have heard the rattle of a cart or carriage spring up suddenly after hours of stillness, and pass, for some minutes, within the range of my hearing as I lay abed. There is a romance about all who are abroad in the black hours, and with something of a thrill we try to guess their business. But here the romance was double : first, this glad passenger, lit internally with wine, who sent up his voice in music through the night ; and then I, on the other hand, buckled into my sack, and smoking alone in the pine-woods between four and five thousand feet towards the stars." (R. L. Stevenson.)

These are both of them good examples of a kind of prose of which it would be easy to give both better and worse instances. The poet even, who when he wishes to speak of playing football and trundling a hoop, will write

> To chase the rolling circle's speed
> Or urge the flying ball :

or describe the champagne at a wedding breakfast as

> The foaming grape of eastern France,

as well as the prose-writer who translates " when we were taken up stairs a dirty fellow bounced out of the bed on which one of us was to lie " into " Out of one of the beds on which we were to repose started up at our entrance a man black as a Cyclops from the forge," or substitutes for " died poor " " expired in indigent circumstances "—are all victims to the desire to decorate, to enhance, to dignify their thought by the manner of saying. For what is it that Jeremy Taylor and Robert Louis Stevenson have done in the passages quoted ? They have added to the effect of a thought or an experience, simple enough in itself, the charm which comes from the suggestion and music, the colour and harmony of words. The thought and the experience has each its emotional value, and the effect of the wording is in part to fix and accentuate this. But in each the art of the writer has gone beyond—it may be fallen short of—this and made of itself, of its own wonderful pattern of vowel and consonant, of word and clause, of sound and colour, a Pan's pipe to enchant us. This style has perhaps the widest range of any, varying from the most playful banter, the decorative badinage, say, of Lamb's essay on roast pig, to the grave and elaborate harmonies of Sir Thomas Browne's *Hydriotaphia* and De Quincey's *Suspiria*, the purple descriptive passages of Ruskin, and the studied and over-precious cadences of Pater's prose. What is common to all is that the style is a garment that will almost stand by itself ; it is a heightening and embellishing of a subject which the writer cannot or does not trust altogether to make its own appeal.

It is this that distinguishes it from the plain style which aims not at attracting attention to itself but to a subject the importance of which, the writer feels, needs only to be insisted on [1] to be recognised. And it distinguishes it equally from what is called the grand style. The grand style is the full development, the complete achievement of the impassioned style, the style whose aim is, according to Cicero, *permovere*, or in Longinus's words, " not persuasion but transport." And the grand style may be as naked or as homely as the plain style. For like the plain style the grand must be rigidly proportioned to its subject— its effect depends on the subject and the form interpenetrating.

Where it differs from the plain style is in the character of the subject or its relation to the mind. The subject of the grand style is a great subject, not necessarily a great subject conceived abstractly, but one that is great to the writer, fraught for him with intense and thrilling significance. The subject of the grand style is a subject *plus* an emotion, and the style is the vehicle by which the emotion is communicated, the subject revealed as transfigured and coloured by the speaker's passionate mood. [2]

[1] The writer recognises that insistence is needed. Emphasis is the object of South's repetitions and illustrations. Herein he differs from the writer of what I have called the colourless style. The latter assumes that his reader is interested in the subject before he opens the book, either through a desire of knowledge or, at the lowest, in order to pass his examination. It is not the author's business either to quicken attention by emphasis or to adorn his subject. But though the plain style is thus by no means colourless, the object of every device is to rivet attention on the theme, not upon itself.

[2] No one has written better on the grand style than the late Professor Saintsbury : *Shakespeare and the Grand Style* and *Dante and the Grand Style*

But passion speaks often in the plainest and the homeliest language. She sometimes cannot speak at all. " The silence of Ajax in the underworld," says Longinus, " is greater and more sublime than words." And again, " The legislator of the Jews, no ordinary man, having formed and expressed a worthy conception of the might of the Godhead writes at the very beginning of His Laws, ' Let there be light, and there was light ; let there be land, and there was land.' " Style has little or nothing to do with the effect here ; the language is as colourless as the statement of a mathematical proposition. But even when coloured, that colour is often homely and plain. There is figure, but that figure is not decorative :

> . . . dove il sol tace

—" the sun which speaks in the silence of noonday ; which suggests its speech by moon and stars in the silence of midnight, is silent, simply and *sans phrase*, in Hell." So Professor Saintsbury comments on half a line of Dante, for Dante excels in these lines of thrilling and overwhelming severity and grandeur. But Shakespeare has them too :

> The wheel is come full circle ; I am here.
>
> A terrible childbed hast thou had, my dear.
>
> The rest is silence.

In prose, too, impassioned writing of the highest quality may be achieved with the aid of the simplest words. Take Bright's great peroration : " I cannot but notice that an uneasy feeling

(*Essays and Studies by Members of the English Association*, 1910, 1912). Now Professor Saintsbury maintains the most thoroughgoing doctrine of the all-important form, separating style from subject at times with a sharpness that reminds one of the Schoolmen. " The cookery is everything," he seems to say, " the original quality of the joint nothing "—a proposition which he would strenuously deny. Accordingly he dwells, quite justly and very instructively, on the contribution made to the total effect of examples of the grand style by all the qualities of words, taken singly or together—meaning, colour, harmony, and rhythm. But at every turn he recognises implicitly and explicitly the determining influence of the subject. Shakespeare, who commands all styles, " knows that to employ a being so majestical for every purpose of a dramatic household is a profanation—that she is for the pageants and the passions, for the big wars and the happy or unhappy loves, for the actions and the agonies of pith and moment."

exists as to the news that may arrive by the very next mail from the East ; I do not suppose that your troops are to be beaten in actual conflict with the foe, or that they will be driven into the sea ; but I am certain that many homes in England in which there now exists a fond hope that the distant one may return— many such homes will be rendered desolate when the next mail shall arrive. The angel of death has been abroad throughout the land ; you may almost hear the beating of his wings. There is no one, as when the first-born was slain of old, to sprinkle with blood the lintel and the two sideposts of our doors, that he may spare and pass on : he takes his victims from the castle of the noble, the mansion of the wealthy, and the cottage of the poor and lowly, and it is on behalf of all these classes that I make this solemn appeal."

The grand style must not be reserved as a title for these shining summits of magnificent simplicity ; or to put it otherwise, the grand style is only the crown and flower of the impassioned and moving style. And the impassioned style is not always simple, far from it. Every resource of the decorative style—and we shall analyse these more fully in the next chapter—is at the command of the impassioned. But even when the impassioned style is clothed in figure and fancy these are generally of a different kind from those of the decorative. They are more plain and homely, drawn from the experiences of everyday life rather than from the lovelier objects of nature and the idealising imagination. When Shakespeare is in the decorative vein he writes as in the early comedies, and in *Romeo and Juliet*, and *Richard II.* :

> It was the lark, the herald of the morn,
> No nightingale : look, love, what envious streaks
> Do lace the severing clouds in yonder east :
> Night's candles are burnt out, and jocund day
> Stands tiptoe on the misty mountain tops.

But in the later tragedies passion speaks in fiercer and homelier, at times even ugly, imagery :

> Lay not that flattering unction to your soul,
> That not your trespass, but my madness speaks :
> It will but skin and film the ulcerous place,
> Whiles rank corruption, mining all within,
> Infects unseen.

Even conceit is not fatal to the language of passion or the grand style. It has generally been condemned on the ground that, as Steele puts it, " deep reflections are made by a head undisturbed ; and points of wit and fancy are the work of a heart at ease." But it is, at any rate in some minds, an effect of passion to quicken the intellect and originate bizarre and subtle strains of reflection. Wild, sinister thoughts are often struck out in the moment of intense agitation :

> If he do bleed,
> I'll gild the faces of the grooms withal,
> For it must seem their guilt.

The splendid sensuality of Cleopatra shines in the conceit in which she dies :

> Dost thou not see my baby at my breast,
> That sucks the nurse asleep ?

Broadly speaking, then, there are these four distinct styles shading off into one another through an infinite series of degrees of colour and rhythm. The question of purity and propriety becomes in consequence not one of asking to which particular fixed class of words each may belong, but what is the tone and colour I must strive to give my treatment of a subject for a special purpose before a special audience actually present or conceived in imagination ? And of almost no word can one say with perfect confidence beforehand that it is suitable for only one of these styles. If in general the plain style is compact of simple words of everyday use it cannot confine itself always to these, while conversely words of the homeliest associations will find their way into not only the passionate but even the decorative style. Words have not only colour in themselves, they take colour from their setting.

CHAPTER IV

FIGURATIVE LANGUAGE

It is a great matter to observe propriety in these several modes of expression—compound words, strange (or rare) words, and so forth. But the greatest thing by far is to have a command of metaphor. This alone cannot be imparted by another ; it is the mark of genius,—for to make good metaphors implies an eye for resemblance.—Aristotle : *Poetics*, xxii. 9.

WHEN we consider, therefore, propriety in the use of words, and recognise that the proper word to use depends upon the kind of style in which we have chosen to treat of our subject, this does not mean that it is possible to draw up in advance lists of words suitable to each of the types of style indicated—the colourless, the plain, the decorative, the impassioned. To do so is not possible to any except a very limited degree, if at all, because the colour of a word is not a fixed quality, it varies to some extent with the use we make of it, the setting in which we place it. If you say " the servant placed the knife upon the table," the word " knife " is either colourless or the associations which it evokes are simple and domestic. But when Lady Macbeth exclaims

> Come, thick night,
> And pall thee in the dunnest smoke of hell,
> That my keen knife see not the wound it makes,
> Nor heaven peep through the blanket of the dark.
> To cry, " Hold, hold ! "

the word " knife " acquires at once a more sinister colour : and so, by the way, does the word " blanket " compared with our everyday use of the word. In plain, unimpassioned writing, such writing as I have called—and the phrase is to be understood relatively, not absolutely—colourless, the colour of the word is latent rather than absent. If one turns back to the passage from Dr Merz, one will note that some of the words are practically colourless, have none but scientific and intellectual associations— " phenomena," " convertibility," " motivity," etc. But others, which in this passage appear sedate and colourless, are capable of producing very different effects, of being made, as it were, to emit colours as vivid and as fluctuating as those of an opal. Compare " had its origin in the early speculations of William Thomson " with

> Thou hast no speculation in those eyes
> Which thou dost glare with.

The first use of the word has, of course, developed from the second, and there is practically a difference of meaning, but even when there is no such difference of meaning one may get difference of colour. Compare " the mechanical view of the phenomena of heat " with

> But he (his musical finesse was such,
> So nice his ear, so delicate his touch)
> Made poetry a mere mechanic art ;
> And every warbler has his tune by heart.

The word " mechanic " or " mechanical " has in the last quotation a suggestion of the disagreeable, acquires, that is, a certain emotional colour. One might illustrate the same capacity to acquire colour in the words " degradation," " dissipation," " calculate," *e.g.* " the calculating mercenary knave."

Words acquire or emit colour according to the degree in which they express and awaken emotion as well as ideas, for colour is merely a metaphor for emotion. But one great effect of emotion on language is to make it figurative, to make the writer or speaker use words in a new and surprising manner that quickens our sense of their emotional significance. The colour of a passage will be found on examination to depend in great measure not simply on the words we choose, but on whether we use them figuratively or not, on what we call the writer's *imagery*. In fact, the general colour or tone of a piece of writing in verse or prose seems to depend on four qualities : (1) the concreteness or abstractness of the language we use, whether the passage deals with concretely presented particulars, or in terms of general, abstract significance ; (2) the figures or images we use. It is the absence of figures, as well as the use of general, abstract terms which gives to a piece of writing like Dr Merz's its colourless appearance. It is the absence of figures, or the use only of those which are simple and homely, that gives to our style " unaffected plainness and simplicity." What South specially denounces in

Jeremy Taylor's style is his "tropes and fine conceits," his "fringes of the North" and "down of angels' wings"; and it is these rich decorative images which make the style of writers like Taylor and Browne and De Quincey and Ruskin a cloth of purple and gold. The third and fourth qualities are (3) structure, simple and idiomatic, or precise and elaborate, and (4) the harmony and rhythm of the words and sentences and paragraphs. Of these we shall have to speak again. The effect of the whole will depend on the harmonious adjustment of all the four factors.

But what are figures of speech? Tropes and figures have bulked so largely in treatises on rhetoric and composition that it seems strange to ask at this late date what they are and why they are used, yet I have never found a work which to my mind gave a simple and satisfactory explanation of their use, showed why and how it was we come thus to extend the range of our vocabulary, to make words play more parts than they were primarily designed for. The ancient writers on rhetoric spoke of them too much as mere ornaments of style, to be added or taken away at will; and were content to make long lists of them with an elaborate nomenclature, and to illustrate their use from poets and orators. They spoke, as Professor Saintsbury has put it, as though the figures were a sugar which you sifted into the pudding in greater or less quantity as you thought well. Their definitions were superficial and left quite unexplained the fact of their being used at all.

For figures of speech are not mere ornaments of style to be used or dispensed with at will. In their origin they are just such natural expressions of emotion as the shedding of tears, or a dog's wagging of its tail. Where they differ from these indications of feeling is in a greater distinctness, in being extensions of the articulate, not merely the inarticulate, expression of our feeling, variations and extensions of the use of language to communicate feeling. We may shed tears for so many different reasons that we need the help of language to convey what is exactly the cause of our shedding tears at any particular moment, and it is in the effort to do this adequately by means of language that we extend the range of language by using it in this figurative fashion. But my meaning will become clearer as I exemplify what I have in view.

The connection of the use of figures of speech with the fundamental laws governing the working of the mind was first indicated

E

by Dr Bain. He pointed out that " a classification of the more important figures may be based on the three leading divisions of the human understanding," namely (1) the feeling of difference, the fact that " the mind is affected by change, as in passing from rest to motion, from cold to heat, from light to dark ; and the greater and more sudden the change, the stronger is the effect " ; (2) the feeling of likeness, agreement—" When like objects come under our notice we are impressed by the circumstance " ; (3) the power of retentiveness, the power of the mind to recall its impressions, which " works in this way : impressions occurring together become associated together, as sunrise with daylight ; and when we are made to think of one, we are reminded of its accompaniments." Metaphor, according to Dr Bain's classification, is a figure of similarity because it depends for its effect upon the natural tendency of the mind to detect likeness even in difference. A pleasurable shock is communicated to the mind by recognising that

> Life's but a walking shadow ; a poor player,
> That struts and frets his hour upon the stage,
> And then is heard no more,

or that two lovers parted yet mindful of each other are like the legs of a pair of compasses :

> Our two souls therefore, which are one,
> Though I must go, endure not yet
> A breach, but an expansion,
> Like gold to airy thinness beate.
>
> If they be two, they are two so
> As stiff twin compasses are two,
> Thy soul, the fixed foot, makes no show
> To move, but doth if th' other do.
>
> And though it in the centre sit,
> Yet when the other far doth roam,
> It leans, and hearkens after it,
> And grows erect, as that comes home.

On the other hand, when we speak of " all *hands* being on deck," or when Peter says " *silver and gold* have I none," or Shylock declares that Portia is " *a Daniel* come to judgment," the law of the human mind on which we count to make our meaning intelligible is that of suggestion. One part of a complex experience is sufficient to recall the rest ; and we receive a shock of pleasure when the really significant detail is brought into relief, just as when a few lines in a caricature bring a whole face and character vividly before us.

Dr Bain's classification is both interesting and important and some of its implications will call for fuller consideration. What it does not explain is, why we come to use figures at all. It is not a sufficient explanation of the damage done to London in an air raid to refer to the law of gravitation which makes bombs fall or that of the expansion of gases which makes them explode, and to make no references to our enemy and their intentions. What we want to know is *why* these forces were so employed. And so it is with figures. It is the end which determines how an instrument is to be used. To appreciate or criticise the use of figures we must apprehend the motives which induce us to devise " forms of speech differing from the common and ordinary modes of expression," to extend in so many ways the significance of the words we use that these words become, like the colours in a painter's box, productive of endless shades of meaning and suggestion.

The ultimate cause is, of course, the desire to communicate our emotions to others. This is the commonest and at the same time the rarest and most difficult, and most rarely achieved, of the ends for which we speak and write. A large number of the statements which we make have a simple utilitarian end in view, as when we tell another the streets he must traverse to reach a certain destination. A smaller number are attempts, more or less accurate, to formulate abstract scientific truths, as that water consists of H_2O, that $(a+b)^2 = a^2 + 2ab + b^2$. In such cases we do not mix our feelings with what we say. But in the far larger number of cases, from an interesting and animated conversation to a poem, the purpose of the speaker or writer is to win sympathy, to communicate facts (if they be facts) or ideas in such a way that his hearers will share the writer's feelings about them. *Hic labor, hoc opus est*—to make another feel as we feel, enter into our hearts and see events and persons and things and ideals through our eyes, that is the ultimate and ineradicable impulse from which have sprung all the arts of expression and perhaps of design. The recurrent tragedy of life is the failure of men to understand one another, their failure in sympathy :

> Yes ! in the sea of life enisled,
> With echoing straits between us thrown,
> Dotting the shoreless watery wild,
> We mortal millions live *alone*.
> The islands feel the enclasping flow,
> And then their endless bounds they know.

Nature has given to us, as to the animals, certain simple and direct means of expressing our feelings [1]—facial expression, gesticulation, tears and laughter, the last two perhaps peculiar to men. And the literary artist avails himself of these, of them all, in dramatic presentation, of exclamation and interjection even in written work. Greek tragedy abounds in such outcries. See, for a striking example, the *Philoctetes* of Sophocles :

> παπαῖ, φεῦ.
> παπαῖ μάλ᾽, ὦ πούς, οἷα μ ἔργασεί κακά—

and when Othello stands over the dead body of Desdemona the culmination of his grief is in exclamation and outcry :

> O Desdemona ! Desdemona ! dead !
> Oh ! Oh ! Oh !

But such means of expression are limited in their range of precise articulation. A few interjections are assigned to pain and grief, others to joy ; and if we know the history of an individual experience we can interpret more closely ; but they do not carry us far. The " infant crying in the night " cries for many reasons. The problem for the nurse, the mother, or the doctor is to discover which is operative.

The means by which, as we gain that mastery of language which reaches its highest manifestation in the work of the great literary artist, we express our feelings with precision is not direct outcry but such a presentation of the cause of our emotion, the subject of our passionate aversion or love or fear, as shall place it vividly before the mind of those whom we address, and not only

---

[1] See Darwin, *Expression of the Emotions in Man and Animals.*

vividly, but so coloured, so transfigured that they shall see it even as we see it, see it through the refracting medium of our impassioned imagination, and so doing share our emotion. To express is to communicate, fully and perfectly.

The first of these means, vivid, concrete presentation of the experience on its objective side, is sometimes, but perhaps not very often, used alone. In many cases it seems to us as if all that were needful is to make our hearers see with their own eyes what we have seen, and they would feel as we do ; and we seek nothing but a burning vividness of presentation ; and our style, if we are successful, acquires that quality which ancient rhetoricians call "enargia." "It is thus," says Quintilian, "that commiseration for captured cities is excited ; for, though he who says that a city is captured doubtless comprehends under that expression all the circumstances with which such a calamity is attended, yet this short kind of announcement makes no impression on the feelings. If you expand, however, what was intimated in the single word, there will be seen flames spreading over houses and temples ; there will be heard the crash of falling edifices, and a confused noise of various outcries ; there will be seen some fleeing, and others clinging in the last embrace of their relatives ; there will be the lamentations of women and children, and old men preserved by an unhappy fate to see that day ; there will be the pillaging of profane and sacred treasures ; the hurrying of soldiers carrying off their booty and seeking for more ; prisoners driven in chains before their captors ; mothers struggling to retain their infants ; and battles among the conquerors wherever the plunder is most inviting. For though, as I have said, the idea of the city being taken includes all these circumstances, yet it is less impressive to tell the whole at once than to specify the different particulars ; and the particulars we shall succeed in making vivid if we but give them a resemblance to the truth." Consider the difference between a brief official despatch from the front and a good correspondent's description of the same operation in detail. Campbell in his *Philosophy of Rhetoric* has another delightful example of the same vivid expansion. "The spring has come" is quite a sufficient statement in most circumstances, including as it does the details of importance to the speaker or hearer. "The spring has come, I shall haul down my boat," "The spring has come, we must

display our light goods," " The spring has come, we must leave
Edinburgh for a warmer climate "—details are unnecessary. But
the lover and the poet are not content with such bare statement,
for what they wish to communicate to you is not the mere fact
but their feeling about the fact. And so you get a description
like this : " My beloved spake, and said unto me, Rise up, my love,
my fair one, and come away. For, lo, the winter is past, the rain
is over and gone ; the flowers appear on the earth ; the time of
the singing of birds is come, and the voice of the turtle is heard
in our land ; the fig tree putteth forth her green figs, and the
vines with the tender grape give a good smell." Again, instead
of saying " in autumn, about the beginning of winter," Browning
writes :

> Well, early in autumn, at first winter warning,
> When the stag had to break with his foot of a morning
> A drinking-hole out of the fresh, tender ice,
> That covered the pond, till the sun in a trice,
> Loosening it let out a ripple of gold,
> And another, another, and faster and faster,
> Till dimpling to blindness the wide water roll'd.

Carlyle writes history with a sustained use of this " enargia,"
setting each scene vividly before your eyes. Macaulay is picturesque,
but with less of movement and fewer dramatic touches. Gibbon,
without being dry or abstract, is content to indicate the larger
features and movements, and his history is in consequence less
dramatic and moving, more panoramic, dignified, and monotonous.

But this is not the only means by which the speaker or writer
communicates feeling with vividness and precision ; nor is it the
device more essentially and peculiarly literary. In the vivid and
detailed portrayal of objective experiences literature will always
fall short of sculpture and the painter's art.[1] And vivid detailed
portraiture *may* fail of its effect. Like the simple and direct forms
of expression referred to above, it may awaken the wrong emotion
or one that has not quite the shade which the writer desires. It
is not enough to make your reader see what you see. He must

---

[1] With the exception which Lessing noted of movement and change ; and
even here the cinematograph suggests a possible extension of the range of
pictorial art beyond the " single moment," though how the artist is to utilise
these means for that expression of emotion which distinguishes art from
mechanical representation is not yet discernible.

see it also in the same light, transfigured by transmission through
the medium of your imagination. And it is just in this that
literature surpasses painting and sculpture, though these arts
too have endeavoured after similar effects and are doing so to-day
perhaps more consciously than ever. By selection and rearrange-
ment, by skilful heightening, by lending to it qualities it does not
objectively possess, as life and personality, and above all by
subtle comparisons, comparisons which have the effect of investing
the object with a colour, a fragrance which was originally not its
but another's, the poet makes his subject something other than
it is in nature, the medium for the communication of his most
intense or most delicate and evanescent feeling, so that the reader
in contemplating the images evoked becomes aware through them
of the life and movement of the poet's soul, and his own soul
trembles in response.

Any piece of good imaginative writing will illustrate these
two qualities of diction. Take Keats's *Ode to Autumn*. The
" mists," the " mellow fruitfulness," " the vines that round the
thatch-eaves run," the swelled gourd and plump " hazel shells "
with their " sweet kernel," the bees and their " clammy cells," the
" barred clouds " that " bloom the soft-dying day "—these and
other phrases all contribute to the " enargia " of the poem, its vivid,
concrete presentation of the changing phases of the season as it
passes from the close of summer to the last clear day that trembles
on the verge of winter :

> and now with treble soft
> The red-breast whistles from a garden-croft ;
> And gathering swallows twitter in the skies.

In the concrete vividness of presentation, the " enargia " of
his description, Keats's poem might be compared with the
description of winter in Shakespeare's *Love's Labour's Lost* :

> When icicles hang by the wall,
>   And Dick the shepherd blows his nail,
> And Tom bears logs into the hall,
>   And milk comes frozen home in pail,
> When blood is nipp'd, and ways be foul,
> Then nightly sings the staring owl—
>   To-whit !
> To-who ! a merry note !
> While greasy Joan doth keel the pot.

> When all aloud the wind doth blow,
>   And coughing drowns the parson's saw,
> And birds sit brooding in the snow,
>   And Marian's nose looks red and raw,
> When roasted crabs hiss in the bowl—
> Then nightly sings the staring owl
>   To-whit !
> To-who ! a merry note !
> While greasy Joan doth keel the pot.

But Shakespeare is here content with the vivid details. His poem is a careless fit of song. Keats's ode is the expression, as its larger, more elaborate rhythms indicate, of a mightier sweep of passionate feeling, and he is *not* content with mere descriptive, vivid, concrete details. As his imagination kindles the subject of contemplation is transfigured. It acquires life and personality. Already the " close bosom-friend of the maturing sun," " conspiring with him " in works of fruitfulness, autumn becomes in the passionate second stanza a shifting series of vividly conceived symbolic personalities, the winnower " sitting careless on the granary floor," the reaper " drows'd with the fume of poppies," the gleaner leaning his " laden head across a brook," the patient presser of cider apples " watching the last oozings hour by hour." And in the subsiding feeling and slowly lapsing rhythms of the closing stanza the season is a soul like that of the poet avid of each last beauty of colour and sound and suggestion.

This is but one example of what one might illustrate indefinitely —the intermingling of concrete, vivid, objective presentation with transfiguring, colouring touches which are the great means of communicating emotion by making our audience see things as vividly and in the same light as we who feel and would communicate our feelings see them. Note the blended objective and transfiguring touches in

> Drug thy memories, lest thou learn it, lest thy heart be put to proof,
> In the dead, unhappy night, and when the rain is on the roof,

the vividness of " when the rain is on the roof," the profound imaginative transfiguration of " dead, unhappy night." Kipling has imitated the effect in his lines :

> When the drunken comrade mutters, and the great guard-lantern gutters,
> And the horror of our fall is written plain,

> Every secret self-revealing on the aching, white-washed ceiling,
> Do you wonder that we drug ourselves from pain ?

" White-washed " is a concrete touch like the muttering of the drunken comrade and the guttering of the lantern. " Aching " adds something more, mixes the speaker's feelings deep into the description, is part of the transfiguring process which has written on these sordid surroundings, as with the finger of God, the horror of the fall.

These two things everyone does who would communicate to others his emotion. He seeks to give vivid objectivity to his experience ; if it has an objective, sensuous source, to describe it as vividly as he may ; if it has not, to give to it something of the character of an objective experience ; but in doing so he mixes his feeling with the description, modifying, colouring, transfiguring it till it becomes the image and symbol of his mental state. And the principal figures of speech are a series of natural but artistically elaborated (for " art is man's nature ") devices, extensions of the use of words, for procuring one or other of these effects.

Consider first some of the ways in which the figurative use of language contributes to vividness of objective presentation, to making more vivid some objective experience or giving to an experience that has its origin in the mind, in thought, the character of an objective, sensuous experience. The little group of figures which rhetoricians call Apostrophe, Exclamation, Vision, serve obviously the purpose of vivid portrayal :

> Now gallant Saxon ! hold thine own !
> No maiden's arm is round thee thrown !
> That desperate grasp thy frame might feel
> Through bars of brass and triple steel !
> They tug, they strain ! down, down they go,
> The Gael above, Fitz-James below.[1]

They are devices for heightening the " enargia " of the description. And they may be used more indirectly to intensify

[1] In his *Rhetoric and Composition*, vol. ii, Dr Bain ascribes these words to Roderick and comments : " In this attitude he can still command a speech, perhaps rather too highly illustrated for reasonable probability in the situation ! " The words are, of course, part of the poet's vivid realisation and description of the incident.

the expression of feeling. When Shakespeare makes Henry personify and apostrophise sleep—

> O sleep ! O gentle sleep !
> Nature's soft nurse, (etc.)

—the " enargia " with which he describes what sleep can do heightens by contrast his sense of the want of sleep.

The same effect of vivid representation is served by the figures which Dr Bain classified under such heads as synecdoche, metonymy. The principle is the same in all. Instead of calling a thing by the ordinary name, which usage has generalised, we name some part or parts, adjunct or adjuncts. Suggestion does the rest, bringing back from the hearer's own experience a more concrete, vivid presentation of the object than the generalised name would.

Instead of saying " It is evening," Gray selects a few striking, typical features from which each of us builds up a detailed picture rich in emotional associations :

> The curfew tolls the knell of parting day ; (etc.)

Tennyson secures the same effect by a single detail :

> Nigh upon that hour,
> When the lone heron forgets his melancholy,
> Lets down his other leg, and stretching, dreams
> Of goodly supper in the distant pool.

In these cases, of course, there is pretty full description of the selected detail or details. More generally there is simply the name of the part selected as picturesque or relevant substituted for the general name of the object or experience referred, but the purpose, vivid concreteness, and the means, suggestion, are the same :

> Bluff Harry broke into the spence
> And turned the *cowls* adrift.

> He carried *fire and sword* through the country.

> The power of the *purse*.

> At length burst in the *argent revelry*
> With plume, tiara, and all rich array.

> He set up Parliaments by the *stroke of his pen* and *scattered them with the breath of his mouth*.

> From the *cradle* to the *grave*.

> Blind *mouths* !

But the great figure for securing both vividness of concrete representation and every kind and degree of emotional transfiguration is the figure of similarity—simile, metaphor, and such varieties as personification, allegory, antonomasia. These have their source in the power of the imagination to discover likenesses in things apparently the most remote from one another, the source of the scientific worker's discovery of new laws, or new applications of laws of nature. For the scientist the differences are quite as important as the resemblances, and it is for him to distinguish by long course of experiment superficial and unimportant from profound and fruitful identities. The artist is more concerned with what appeals to the senses and touches the emotions, yet the greatness of a poet too is measurable by the real significance of the resemblances on which he builds, the depth of their roots in the constitution, if not of the physical world, of the moral and emotional nature of man.[1]

The primary object of many similes and metaphors is to secure concreteness of description beyond that which any single word with its generalised significance can procure. So Thomson speaks of the " wallflower's iron brown " and Tennyson of hair

> More black than ashbuds in the front of March.

Burns's poetry abounds in such vivid, concrete similes and metaphors :

> An' thy auld hide as white's a daisie . . .
> Tho' now ye dow but hoyte and hoble,
> An' wintle like a saumont-coble.

The same effect is secured by more elaborate similes : " Even as when the tribes of thronging bees issue from some hollow rock, ever in fresh procession, and fly clustering among the flowers of spring, and some on this hand and some on that

---

[1] This is the significance of the distinction which Coleridge and Wordsworth laboured between Fancy and Imagination. To aggregate and to associate, to evoke and to combine, belong as well to the imagination as to the fancy ; but either the materials evoked and combined are different, or they are brought together under a different law, and for a different purpose. One might say that fancy in poetry corresponds to the first tendency of observers to call whales fish ; imagination to the deeper view which identifies them with mammals.

fly thick ; even so from ships and huts before the low beach marched forth their many tribes by companies to the place of assembly." And in imitation of this, Milton's

> As bees
> In spring-time, when the Sun with Taurus rides,
> Pour forth their populous youth about the hive
> In clusters ; they among fresh dews and flowers
> Fly to and fro, or on the smoothed plank,
> The suburb of their straw-built citadel,
> New rubb'd with balm, expatiate and confer
> Their state-affairs : so thick the aery crowd
> Swarm'd and were straiten'd.

> Mid the sharp short *emerald* wheat, scarce risen three finger well,
> The wild tulip, at end of its tube, blows out its great red *bell*
> Like a *thin clear bubble of blood*, for the children to pick and smell.

But this is not the only way in which similes and metaphors give concreteness of effect. Under the influence of emotion the almost irresistible tendency of the mind is to give to subjective experiences, to thoughts and complex states of mind, the character of sensible experiences, and it is by the aid of simile and metaphor that this is achieved :

" I never heard the old song of Percy and Douglas, that I found not my heart moved *more than with a trumpet*."

> Love is flower-like,
> Friendship is *a sheltering tree*.

> For I am as a *weed*,
> *Flung from the rock*, on ocean's foam to sail
> Where'er the surge may sweep, the tempest's breath prevail.

The test of the degree to which a thought is dear to the heart of him who utters it, is native to his very soul, may be found in the degree to which he tends to clothe its expression in concrete, sensible imagery. When Burns is talking merely from the intellectual side of his nature, or moved by some superficial mood of anger, he declaims in generalisation or frigid personifications :

> Look not alone on youthful prime,
>   Or manhood's active might ;
> Man then is useful to his kind,
>   Supported is his right ;

> But see him on the edge of life,
>   With cares and sorrows worn ;
> Then age and want—oh ! ill-match'd pair—
>   Show man was made to mourn.

When the current of passion is flowing strongly through his soul, when he is uttering the inmost man, he clothes his thought in glowing imagery :

> But why o' death begin a tale,
> Just now we're livin' sound and hale ;
> Then top and maintop crowd the sail,
>   Heave care o'er-side,
> And large before enjoyment's gale
>   Let's tak' the tide.

To find the genuine pessimist, the soul sensitive to melancholy to its inmost fibre, we have but to turn to Carlyle and note the imagery in which he pours forth his feelings : " The tomb is now my inexpugnable fortress : O ye loved ones that already sleep in the noiseless bed of rest, whom in life I could only weep for, never help ; and ye who widely scatter'd still toil lonely in the monster-bearing desert, dyeing the thirsty ground with your blood ; yet a little while and we shall all meet there, and our mother's bosom will screen us all ; and oppression's harness and sorrow's fire-whip and all the Gehenna-bailiffs that patrol and inhabit ever vexed time cannot henceforth harm us any more." When the same author would make us see clearly and feel strongly what seems to him the unnatural and dangerous economic condition of the nation, he describes in a couple of vivid images what it would take an elaborate series of abstract, generalised statements to define with precision :

" I could liken Dandyism and Drudgism to two bottomless boiling Whirlpools that had broken-out on opposite quarters of the firm land : as yet they appear only disquieted, foolishly bubbling wells, which man's art might cover-in ; yet mark them, their diameter is daily widening : they are hollow Cones that boil-up from the infinite Deep, over which your firm land is but a thin crust or rind ! Thus daily is the intermediate land crumbling-in, daily the empire of the two Buchan-Bullers extending ; till now there is but a foot-plank, a mere film of Land between them ; this too is washed away : and then—we have the true Hell of Waters, and Noah's Deluge is outdeluged !

" Or better, I might call them two boundless, and indeed unexampled Electric Machines (turned by the ' Machinery of Society '), with batteries of opposite quality ; Drudgism the Negative, Dandyism the Positive : one attracts hourly towards it and appropriates all the Positive Electricity of the nation (namely, the Money thereof) ; the other is equally busy with the Negative (that is to say the Hunger), which is equally potent. Hitherto you see only partial transient sparkles and sputters : but wait a little, till the entire nation is in an electric state ; till your whole vital Electricity, no longer healthfully Neutral, is cut into two isolated portions of Positive and Negative (of Money and of Hunger) ; and stands there bottled-up in two World-Batteries ! The stirring of a child's finger brings the two together ; and then —what then ? The Earth is but shivered into impalpable smoke by that Doom's-thunderpeal ; the Sun misses one of his Planets in Space, and thenceforth there are no eclipses of the Moon."

The primary purpose of such figures is, as I have said, to heighten the vividness of description, the description of what moves us, on which depends in part the expression, the communication of our feelings, which is the directing end of literature as a fine art. But it is seldom the sole purpose ; and indeed this vivid presentation is often secured with but little help from simile or metaphor, by well-selected, significant details, by felicitous epithets. Take one or two examples at random, noting the purely concrete touches :

> *All was silent, all was gloom,*
> *Abroad* and *in the homely room :*
> *Down she sat,* poor cheated soul !
> And *struck a lamp from the dismal coal ;*
> *Lean'd forward,* with *bright drooping hair*
> And *slant book, full against the glare.*
> Her shadow, *in uneasy guise,*
> *Hover'd about, a giant size,*
> On *ceiling-beam* and *old oak chair,*
> The *parrot's cage,* and *panel square ;*
> And the *warm angled winter screen,*
> On which were *many monsters* seen,
> Call'd *doves of Siam, Lima mice,*
> And *legless birds of Paradise,*

> *Macaw*, and *tender Avadavat*,
> And *silken-furr'd Angora cat*.
> Untir'd she read, her *shadow still*
> *Glower'd about, as it would fill*
> *The room with wildest forms and shades*,
> *As though some ghostly queen of spades*
> *Had come to mock behind her back*,
> *And dance*, and *ruffle her garments black*.

The vividness and the emotional tone of Keats's poem depend to a great extent on the selection, and description of the details selected, in this picture, but there are very few figures. The "dismal coal" is one, but its effect is not concrete and sensible, at least directly. "Hover'd about, a giant size" is another; and at the end the writing grows more boldly figurative.

The something more than concrete vividness which the simile or metaphor adds is a varying degree of transfiguration. It may be very little, it may be a complete transformation, but the end is always the same—to reveal the aspect which things bear to the heated imagination of the speaker. In Thomson's "iron brown" there is probably nothing more than the shade of colour indicated, yet the contact in the imagination of iron and a flower generates something of a picturesque halo that would be lost in an adjective—if there were one—naming the exact shade. And this picturesque halo, this atmosphere of sensuous beauty, is very obvious in the Tennysonian and Homeric similes, while Burns's "wintle like a saumont-coble" is more than merely descriptive, it is touched with humour. And this intermixture of modifying, transfiguring feeling is found in every simile, the test at once of the writer's power of subtle expression and the reader's delicacy of appreciation. Milton's most elaborate similes are a study in the rendering of moods. Note the different shades of the three figures in the following, whose primary purpose is again vivid description :

> he stood, and call'd
> His legions, Angel Forms, who lay entranc'd
> Thick as autumnal leaves that strow the brooks
> In Vallombrosa, where the Etrurian shades
> High overarch'd embower ; or scatter'd sedge
> Afloat, when with fierce winds Orion arm'd
> Hath vex'd the Red Sea coast, whose waves o'erthrew
> Busiris and his Memphian chivalry,

> While with perfidious hatred they pursu'd
> The sojourners of Goshen, who beheld
> From the safe shore their floating carcases
> And broken chariot-wheels, so thick bestrown,
> Abject and lost lay these, covering the flood,
> Under amazement of their hideous change.

The effect of the first figure is, like the Homeric ones quoted above, purely picturesque, an expression of the poet's love of beauty indulged even when the subject hardly seems to invite it. With the second an angrier hue begins to be diffused through the pictures, as the host takes to the mind's eye the appearance of being scattered like weeds after a terrible storm. With the third— for it is a distinct comparison though by a fine " turn " it is brought in as part of the second—the feeling grows intenser still, the Hebraic hatred of the Egyptian host passes into Milton's description of the lost angels. The description becomes indeed even more realistic, but passionate exultation over their deserved overthrow has become the dominant mood, mixed into the picture like a lurid colour.

But such elaborately wrought-out similes are rare except in the decorative and grand style of epic poetry. In dramatic and lyric poetry and in prose the vivid and transfiguring touches are conveyed in a word, often or at most a briefly developed comparison. The feeling through which the speaker sees what he speaks of and would convey to us plays in and out of his words like the shifting lights and colours of shot silk :

" He was the first poet I ever knew. His genius at that time *had angelic wings*, and *fed on manna*. He talked on for ever. His thoughts did not seem to come with labour and effort, but as if *borne on the gusts of genius*, and as if *the wings of imagination lifted him from off his feet*. His voice *rolled* on the ear *like the pealing organ*. His mind was *clothed with wings* ; and *raised on them* he *lifted philosophy to heaven*. In his descriptions you then saw the progress of human happiness and liberty in bright and never-ending succession, *like the steps of Jacob's ladder, with airy steps ascending and descending, and with the voice of God at the top of the ladder*." A passage like this gives no concrete description of Coleridge's conversation, yet suggests its character in a wonderful way by figures that show it us through its effect on Hazlitt's mind, and in order to convey that impression Hazlitt accumulates comparisons with experiences on whose power to elevate he can count, from a knowledge of the associations which have gathered around them for himself and his audience.

For it is on this that the modifying, transfiguring effect depends. The colour which our images communicate depends on the source from which we draw them. In a purely descriptive comparison, we bring together things of similar objective qualities—brown hair and chestnuts, gold hair and fields of grain—

> The hair that lay along her back
> Was yellow like ripe corn—

tulips and the colour of blood. In transfiguring similes and metaphors the connecting link is *not* in the things themselves but in our feeling about them, the associations with which our experience has invested them. When Burns sings

> O, my Luve's like a red, red rose
> That's newly sprung in June,

he is not describing the colour of her cheeks. He is investing her with the charm and fragrance that roses have for him and for us. And when Wordsworth says of Milton

> Thy soul was like a Star, and dwelt apart,

he is not describing vividly the loneliness of Milton's life—Milton was a passionate politician—but investing with sublimity the transcendent purity of the motives which guided him.

The range of effects at the poet's command is just as wide as his experience and as that of the audience, real or ideal, which he is addressing. All that men know and which has gathered about it human associations, which experience has made for them lovely or sublime or hateful, which familiarity has made " dear "—in the Elizabethan sense of the word, *i.e.* acutely felt as pleasurable or painful—these are the colours on the poet's palette, which he uses and mingles as his genius directs, to give to things the hues which communicate the value that they have for him.[1]

[1] A common source, at all times, of effective, lively, sometimes thrilling metaphors is the sports which are in vogue. Shakespeare's plays abound

F

Compare the imagery of some of Shakespeare's earlier comedies with that of his later tragedies, and note how much the colour depends on the sources from which he draws his images. In the former he revels in all that is picturesque and charming—Ovidian mythology, the beauties of flowers and colours ; in the latter the most thrilling effects are due to the imaginative use of familiar, poignant experiences. Compare

> Then, if he lose, he makes a swan-like end,
> Fading in music : that the comparison
> May stand more proper, my eye shall be the stream
> And watery death-bed for him. He may win,

in figurative allusions to hunting and hawking. (See *The Diary of Master William Silence*, The Right Hon. D. H. Madden, London, 1897 ; and such other studies of Shakespeare's imagery as Caroline F. Spurgeon's *Shakespeare's Imagery and what it tells us*, Cambridge, 1935 ; and Wolfgang Clemen, *Shakespeares Bilder*, etc., Bonn, 1936.) Speaking of Beatrice in *Much Ado*, Benedick says : " I would my horse had the speed of your tongue, and so good a continuer. But keep your way i' God's name ; I have done." Over Julius Cæsar's dead body Antony exclaims :

> Here wast thou bay'd, brave hart ;
> Here didst thou fall ; and here thy hunters stand,
> Sign'd in thy spoil, and crimson'd in thy lethe.

Of Desdemona, when his suspicions have been excited, Othello cries in his anguish and anger :

> If I do prove her haggard,
> Though that her jesses were my dear heart-strings,
> I'd whistle her off, and let her down the wind
> To prey at fortune.

" A haggard is a wild hawk which has lived and fared at liberty untill she has moulted for the first time and has assumed her adult plumage. . . . But though the wild falcon makes the best hawk when manned and trained, the haggard unreclaimed (untamed) is the type of worthlessness and inconstancy " (Madden). It is just so that Othello will deem of Desdemona. In these figures, as in others, it is the *feeling* which has gathered round the sport that is transferred to a new object. Such figures abound, not only in literature, but in the speech of every day : " to turn tail," " to prick up one's ears," " a dead heat," " a slow coach." Such figures, and scores more, are found in everyday speech more or less effectively used because people say what interests them. The one style which you will seldom hear in conversation is the colourless. The so-called slang of the Americans consists largely of racy metaphors taken from the experiences of every day.

> And what is music then ? then music is
> Even as the flourish when true subjects bow
> To the new-crowned monarch : such it is
> As are those dulcet sounds in break of day
> That creep into the dreaming bridegroom's ear
> And summon him to marriage,

with

> To-morrow, and to-morrow, and to-morrow,
> Creeps in this petty pace from day to day,
> To the last syllable of recorded time ;
> And all our yesterdays have lighted fools
> The way to dusty death.   Out, out, brief candle !
> Life's but a walking shadow ; a poor player,
> That struts and frets his hour upon the stage,
> And then is heard no more : it is a tale
> Told by an idiot, full of sound and fury,
> Signifying nothing.

The transfiguring, colouring effect of such similitudes is very clearly seen in two figures, of which one is just a special class of metaphor, the other a vivid reflection of the speaker's strong feeling. To *personify*, to give life and character to things inanimate or abstract, and to *exaggerate* are two of the commonest effects of passionate feeling.[1] There are no two figures, accordingly, which represent more obviously the influence of the mind's feeling on what it communicates. No one would for a moment

---

[1] Wordsworth, whose desire was to identify the language of poetry with the natural language of emotion, recognises this. Professor Saintsbury, indeed, states that Wordsworth " utterly refuses Personification " (*History of Criticism*, iii, 203). But this is a mistake. What Wordsworth " refuses " is frigid, conventional, traditional personifications. His own words are quite explicit : " The reader will find that personifications of abstract ideas rarely occur in these volumes ; and are utterly rejected as an ordinary device to elevate the style and raise it above prose. My purpose was to imitate and as far as is possible to adopt the very language of men ; and assuredly such personifications do not make any natural or regular part of that language. They are, indeed, a figure of speech occasionally prompted by passion, and I have made use of them as such ; but have endeavoured utterly to reject them as a mechanical device of style, or as a family language which writers in metre seem to lay claim to by prescription."

But some accounts of miracles would seem to be traceable to a later hardening of hyperbolical personification into a supposed historical narrative, *e.g.* the standing still of the sun (Joshua x. 12-13).

imagine that the poet of the Psalms is describing vividly objective experiences when he writes :

> The sea saw it and fled : Jordon was driven back.
> The mountains skipped like rams, and the little hills like lambs.
> What ailed thee, O thou sea, that thou fleddest ?
>   Thou Jordan, that thou wast driven back ?
> Ye mountains, that ye skipped like rams ; and ye little hills, like lambs ?
> Tremble, thou earth, at the presence of the Lord, at the presence of the God of Jacob.

In a passage like this hyperbole and personification go together. The Psalms, and oriental poetry generally, abound in such passages. But personification is not always so obviously hyperbolical. It partakes more of the nature of a felicitous and elaborated simile with the touch of life which passion communicates. In the fourteenth ode of the first book Horace compares the state to a ship on a stormy sea, and so far you have a happy simile, but his passionate anxiety adds life to the ship and he apostrophises it :

> O Navis, referent in mare te novi
> Fluctus ! O quid agis ?   Fortiter occupa
>   Portum !   Nonne vides ut
>   Nudum remigio latus,
>
> Et malus celeri saucius Africo,
> Antennaeque gemant, ac sine funibus
>   Vix durare carinae
>   Possint imperiosius
> Aequor ?

Contemplating the history of Oxford and the beauty of her dreaming towers and gardens steeped in moonlight, Arnold sees her as a Queen of Romance waging ceaseless war with Philistinism. And Edinburgh, stripped of her walls, and her streets and houses flowing down into the new town, is compared by Scott to Britomart disarming :

> When, placed at rest,
> What time she was Malbecco's guest,
> She gave to flow her maiden vest ;
> When from her corslet's grasp relieved
> Free to the sight her bosom heaved ;
> And down her shoulders graceful roll'd
> Her locks profuse, of paly gold.

> They who whilom in midnight fight
> Had marvell'd at her matchless might,
> No less her maiden charms approved,
> But looking liked, and liking loved.

Such personifications are just similes with this special vivifying touch. In other cases the process goes further, shaping a fresh and detailed figure and character expressive of the influence of the experience, the object personified in the writer's spirit. Such personifications, symbolic figures, *e.g.* Death, become frequently traditional, and in the modifications which they undergo one can trace the changing moods of the mind of man.

Hyperbole reflects in the same way the transfiguring effect of passion. We paint things not as they are objectively or normally but so as to reflect their value for us :

> Was this the face that launched a thousand ships
> And burn'd the topless towers of Ilion ?

" I thought ten thousand swords must have leapt from their scabbards to avenge even a look that threatened her with insult. . . . But the age of chivalry is gone. That of sophisters, economists and calculators has succeeded ; and the glory of Europe is extinguished for ever."

> Will all great Neptune's ocean wash this blood
> Clean from my hand ? Nay ; this my hand will rather
> The multitudinous seas incarnadine,
> Making the green one red.

The question of the truthfulness of such writing must always be taken as relating to truth of feeling. Do the words reflect what the speaker feels ? and is what he feels extravagant or does it represent what human nature would or should feel if men clearly realised the circumstances ?

The so-called figures of contrast—antithesis, epigram, irony—do not result in the same way from the vivifying and transfiguring effect of feeling in what we are describing. They are figures rather in the wide sense in which some of the ancient rhetoricians used the word when they tried to bring under this head every striking and unusual form of phrasing. Antithesis is simply the explicit statement for the sake of emphasis of the opposite implied in your assertion. " Two men I honour and no third," " The letter killeth, but the spirit giveth life."

Irony is a subtler use of contrast. You state the opposite of what you mean, leaving something in the tone of your statement or its relation to the known facts to suggest your real meaning. The effect is an illumination of the speaker's feeling, not by the revelation of his subject in a more vivid or a transfiguring light, but by the peculiar angle which is presented between the object and the speaker's mind. " No doubt ye are the people and wisdom shall die with you," says Job, and the tone in which he says it, the interval between the statement and the facts of the case, open a window through which we see into his lacerated mind. And it is wounded, angry feeling that most often finds expression in this indirect yet vivid fashion :

> My love, she's but a lassie yet,
>   My love, she's but a lassie yet ;
> We'll let her stand a year or twa,
>   She'll no be half sae saucy yet.
> We're a' dry wi' drinkin' o't,
>   We're a' dry wi' drinkin' o't ;
> The minister kissed the fiddler's wife
>   And could'na preach for thinkin' o't.

The greatest master of irony who used the English language was the man who had inscribed on his tomb the dreadful words that death had taken him " ubi saeva indignatio ulterius cor lacerare nequit." But anger is not the only passion that utters itself in irony. A lofty sense of sorrow, a consciousness of the interval which separates human life as it is from human life as it might be, is the inspiration of some of the greatest writing the world knows in the Bible, in Plato, and in Pascal. And a passion of grief in which is no admixture of anger at all colours the sublime modera-tion, the piercing simplicity of Othello's last words :

> Soft you ; a word or two before you go.
> I have done the state some service, and they know't ;—
> No more of that.—I pray you, in your letters,
> When you shall these unlucky deeds relate,
> Speak of me as I am ; nothing extenuate,
> Nor set down aught in malice ; then must you speak
> Of one that lov'd not wisely, but too well ;

Of one not easily jealous, but, being wrought,
Perplex'd in the extreme ; of one whose hand,
Like the base Indian, threw a pearl away
Richer than all his tribe ; of one whose subdu'd eyes,
Albeit unused to the melting mood,
Drop tears as fast as the Arabian trees
Their medicinable gum.   Set you down this ;
And say, besides,—that in Aleppo once,
Where a malignant and a turban'd Turk
Beat a Venetian and traduc'd the state,
I took by the throat the circumcised dog,
And smote him—thus.

A clear apprehension of the main figures of speech as artistic developments of the natural language of emotion is the surest guide to their right use, and the surest indication of the impossibility of giving any practical rules that are of universal validity.   There are no ready-reckoners, no short-cuts for the man who would write well.   A wide command of his medium, a clear comprehension of his purpose, a steady insight into the character of the audience real or ideal which he is addressing—these are his guiding stars ; but to sail by them he must rely on his own knowledge and tact.

A common rule, for example, bids you avoid mixed metaphors. But intensity of feeling and a rapid flow of ideas will often produce a huddle of images which, if not logically consistent, are very effective.   One may carry too far the rule of consistency in the details of a metaphor, for the point of contact, of resemblance, may be so slight that any elaboration will destroy the illuminating or transfiguring effect.   The rapid transition to another appropriate metaphor may do more to heighten the original tone.   Shakespeare says " to take arms against a sea of troubles," and the effect would only be weakened by changing " sea " to " host " for the sake of consistency.   Pope is not so happy, for there is more of intellectual neatness than of emotional tumult, in his rapid succession of metaphors : [1]

At length Erasmus
Stemm'd the wild torrent of a barbarous age,
And drove the holy Vandals off the stage.

---

[1] An extreme example of a mixed metaphor has been pointed out to me in Mark Pattison's *Memoirs* :   " Even at this day a country squire or rector, on *landing* with his *cub* under his *wing* in Oxford, finds himself *at sea.*"

The tumultuous succession of metaphors which may threaten to cross and blend with each other is itself the index of the passionate mood. It is easy for Dr Bain to criticise Macbeth's speech :

> Besides, this Duncan
> Hath borne his faculties so meek, hath been
> So clear in his great office, that his virtues
> Will plead like angels, trumpet-tongued, against
> The deep damnation of his taking-off ;
> And pity, like a naked new-born babe,
> Striding the blast, or heaven's cherubin, hors'd
> Upon the sightless couriers of the air,
> Shall blow the horrid deed in every eye,
> That tears shall drown the wind.

It is easy to say in a cool hour that these metaphors are extravagant and chaotic. The question is, are they not a vivid reflex of a sensitive, superstitious, visionary mind as it wakes to a sense of guilt, before the fatal Rubicon has yet been crossed ?

Images to be effective must be the expression of feeling, the more exact the better. The worst fault in their use is to use them mechanically, conventionally, frigidly. This is the vice of the worst kind of journalistic writing and stump oratory—the use of metaphors which have lost all freshness and vitality, which are kept on stock, ready for use on every occasion. This was the vice of eighteenth-century poetic style against which Wordsworth's preface was a protest, a protest awkwardly elaborated, and marred by serious but very natural and explicable blunders. Wordsworth in revolt from the artifice appealed to nature. For poetic language, if this was poetic language, he would substitute the language that men actually use under the influence of strong feeling. And he was quite right. Poetic language has its ultimate source in the natural expression of feeling. We are all at moments poets when deeply moved. But if artifice is the antithesis of nature, art is its fulfilment. The language of poetry is not to be acquired by simply noting and recording the actual expressions of men under the influence of feeling. For but few of us are able to find adequate expression for our feelings. Under the influence of feeling most of us are as infants

> crying in the night,
> And with no language but a cry.

The poet looks within. He has the gift of utterance. His language is the completion and perfection of our stammerings.

And the other error in the use of imagery is extravagance —the use of figures which are in excess of what we feel. Conventionality and extravagance go hand in hand. We escape from the outworn into meaningless hyperbole. To describe Mrs Delaney's paper representations of flowers Darwin mingles hackneyed epithets and extravagant personifications :

> Now Delaney forms her *mimic* bowers,
> Her paper foliage and her silken flowers ;
> With virgin train the tender scissors plies,
> And the green leaf, the purple petal dyes.

CHAPTER V

THE DICTION OF POETRY

Poesis est ars exquisite inveniendi et exquisite dicendi quod inveneris.
—Boccaccio.

I HAVE tried to show in the last chapter that the purpose which the imaginative, emotional writer has in view, whether his medium be verse or prose, determines certain essential characteristics of his diction—especially what I have called concreteness and transfiguration, the vivid, objective presentation of what moves him, and the presentation of that object as refracted by transmission through his imagination. The transfiguration is of many kinds, and is often subtly blended with what seems to aim at nothing but vivid concrete description, adds touches the effect of which is to invest the description with an atmosphere derivable from the associations that it brings with it :

> The hair that lay along her back
> Was yellow like ripe corn,

might have been, as far as the *colour* alone is concerned, " yellow as ripe cheese." Compare Butler's

> And, like a lobster boil'd, the morn
> From black to red began to turn.

That is quite vivid, but Rossetti in the lines cited is aiming at something more than accuracy and vividness of description. He is investing the hair with an atmosphere which derives from his own feelings, appealing to our consciousness of the beauty of a cornfield. So in Tennyson's

> her hair
> In gloss and hue the chestnut when the shell
> Divides threefold to show the fruit within ;

but Tennyson's description, if more discriminating as description of the colour, is not emotionally so effective as Rossetti's.

Sometimes the effect the poet has in view besides accurate

description is not so obviously emotional as in the above but rather decorative, to suggest beauty.   Consider Chaucer's cock :

> His comb was finer than the red coral,
> And battailed as it were a castle wal.
> His bil was blak, and as the jet it shoon,
> Like asure were his legges and his toon ;
> His nailes whiter than the lilie flour,
> And like the burned gold was his colour.

That is vivid description, because every detail is objectively valid. But the suggested comparisons with the battlements of a castle wall, and burnished gold, and the lily flower add decoration to the vivid details.   But compare Chaucer's lines with some from Spenser's *Epithalamion*, and note how much further the emotional poet may go in decoration of the object of his feelings :

> Tell me, ye merchants' daughters, did ye see
> So faire a creature in your towne before ?
> So sweet, so lovely, and so mild as she,
> Adornd with beauties grace and vertues store :
> Her goodly eyes like saphyres shining bright,
> Her forehead yvory white,
> Her cheeks like apples which the sun hath rudded,
> Her lips lyke cherreyes charming men to byte,
> Her brest like to a bowle of cream uncrudded,
> Her paps lyke lyllies budded,
> Her snowie necke like to a marble towre,
> And all her body like a palace fayre,
> Ascending uppe with many a stately stayre
> To honours seat and chastities sweet bowre.

Every detail is not only vivid but invested with all the charm that the different things used by way of comparison have already for us—sapphires, ivory, apples, cherries, cream, lilies, marble, a palace, stately stairs.   A suggestion of beauty clings about the individual words.   (See *Words and Poetry*, by George H. W. Rylands (1928).)

Of course, if beauty is not the effect you wish to produce but, it may be, pathos or horror, you will use quite different sources for your transfiguring metaphors :

> Ah ! dear Juliet,
> Why art thou yet so fair ?   Shall I believe
> That unsubstantial Death is amorous,

> And that the lean abhorred monster keeps
> Thee here in dark to be his paramour ?
> For fear of that I still will stay with thee,
> And never from this palace of dim night
> Depart again : here, here will I remain
> With worms that are thy chambermaids ; O, here
> Will I set up my everlasting rest,
> And shake the yoke of inauspicious stars
> From this world-wearied flesh.—Eyes, look your last !
> Arms, take your last embrace ! and lips, O you
> The doors of breath, seal with a righteous kiss
> A dateless bargain to engrossing death !—
> Come, bitter conduct, come, unsavoury guide !
> Thou desperate pilot, now at once run on
> The dashing rocks thy sea-sick weary bark !

Here the lover's feelings overflow in a series of personifications and metaphors drawn from not decorative but emotional or potentially moving experiences.   Juliet has become the paramour of Death pictured, as always by Shakespeare, in the form of a skeleton.   The tomb has become a palace, but one where night inhabits.   The chambermaids are worms.   The lover is throwing his last stake in desperation.   Life and fate, governed by the stars—

> it is the stars,
> The stars above us, govern our condition,

—have become for Romeo a yoke with its associations of slavery and toil, a yoke which he will throw off.   He is a pilot running the ship, which is his life, upon the rocks—a ship which has grown weary of itself, made seasick by the tossing billows of life.

All this is the language of feeling and some of it might be used by a writer in prose.   What, then, do we mean by poetic diction ? Two things, I think.   In the first place, the poet claims, and is allowed, a bolder use of such language than is generally expected from the prose-writer.   At times, indeed, there has been a deliberate cultivation of what is called poetical prose.   But just as such prose though rhythmical does not become metrical, so there are boldnesses in the use of metaphor, personification, hyperbole, and striking departures from the normal in idiom and order of words, which we expect to find accompanied by the form or pattern of verse, or whatever in any language is accepted as the recognised pattern of poetry.

But the phrase " poetic diction " is used often in a more limited sense to indicate a recurring phenomenon of poetry in some languages, certainly in English : the use, namely, of certain words, phrases, grammatical forms, syntactical turns of expression, which are confined to verse-writing, used only along with what is accepted as the pattern of poetry—metre and rhyme, stress and alliteration, etc. Dr Bain's *Grammar* used to tell us in my day that the pronoun " thou " was obsolete except " in addressing the Almighty " and " in poetical use." You will have remarked that modern poets tend to reject it for the colloquial " you." There are other grammatical forms which we accept, or did so till lately, as permissible in poetry though not current.

Aristotle in the *Poetics* classifies the words that are at the disposal of the poet, and his classification fairly well covers the ground for English poetry too. There are (1) current words, which include compound words of two kinds : those of " a significant and a non-significant part " (as " compound " itself) and those composed of " two significant words," as " stone-wall " (the poets have always allowed themselves to coin compounds of this last kind, *e.g.* Spenser's " sea-shouldering whales " which delighted the youthful Keats, etc., etc.) ; (2) strange or foreign words ; in English largely Latin, but also French and Italian and Spanish, and even from remoter sources in modern poets : (3) metaphor, under which we may include the whole of figurative language such as we have discussed above, allowing to the poet a bolder use ; (4) ornamental, which he does not define (such a word would probably come also under either " foreign " or the next class) ; (5) coined words, in the use of which Spenser abounds and Keats allows himself great liberty, and most of our poets indulge. (See Mr Pearsall Smith's interesting studies of those who have thus enriched our tongue, for not infrequently the poet's creation becomes in time a current word.) Of one special feature of the English language the poets have taken advantage, for good and for ill : " The faculty," says Jespersen, " of using one and the same form with different values, while the context shows in most cases unmistakably what part of speech is meant, is one of the most characteristic traits of English, and is found to a similar extent in no other European language." Think of Shakespeare's " You shall *nose* him as you go up the stairs " and " Com'st thou to *beard* me here in Denmark ? " Keats was criticised for the abuse of this licence in lines such as :

> In that same void white Chastity shall sit,
> And *monitor* me nightly to lone slumber,

and even in *Hyperion* :

> the laden heart
> Is persecuted more, and fever'd more,
> When it is *nighing* to the mournful house
> Where other hearts are sick of the same bruise,

where the bold use is in " nighing," for " fever'd " and " bruise " are licensed as both nouns and verbs ; (6) words lengthened, curtailed, or otherwise altered, to put Aristotle's three classes into one. A simple instance is our past in " -ed," which when possible we slur. In older texts it is to be pronounced if printed (barring errors), and Milton is careful to indicate the slurrings by his spelling :

> Uninterrupted joy, unrivall'd love.

We have grown so used to printing the " -ed " but slurring it in speaking that a fastidious poet will accent the " -èd," if he wishes it to be pronounced. This class will include most of the examples of older forms used for poetical purpose by Spenser and other poets.

There are varieties within each of these groups which will show themselves when you study the diction of this or that poet : for example, foreign words become part and parcel of the language but often in a modified or restricted meaning. Then what the poet does often effectively is to use the word in its original sense rather than in that which it has acquired : so Milton in

> on th'Aleian field I fall
> *Erroneous* there to wander, and forlorn,

or " with serpent *errour* wandering."

After discussing these classes of words, Aristotle makes a remark which also has interest for our examination of English poetical diction : " Of the kinds of words we have enumerated it may be observed that compounds are most in place in the dithyramb, strange words in heroic, and metaphors in iambic poetry. Heroic poetry, indeed, may avail itself of them all. But in iambic verse, which models itself as far as possible on the spoken language, only those kinds which are allowable in an oration, *i.e.* the metaphor, the ordinary word and the ornamental equivalent." What emerges from a study of the use of a poetical vocabulary in this narrower sense is this : The poetic vocabulary is at once an opportunity for the poet and a concession to his difficulties. It is a means by which he can give to his style what Wyld calls a " sense of remoteness and augustness," and do so when the more ordinary words would recall prosaic associations. Some words have proved very difficult for poets, *e.g.* " moustache " or " whiskers." You find Spenser accordingly writing :

> And his sweet lips, on which before that stound
> The bud of youth to blossom fair began,

and Tennyson later speaks of :

> The knightly growth that fringed his lip.

On the other hand the use of a poetical vocabulary, as it grows stereotyped, is a help to the poet if he has to use a very elaborate metrical pattern. This is the case in most early poetry, which is also often the work of a school of poets, even if only one genius among them have survived in anything more than a name. The Homeric hexameter is a more elaborate form than the iambic of the dramatists, as what Aristotle says above indicates. Accordingly the diction is more archaic and " poetical," abounding in words of which we do not even know for certain the meaning. So Old English or Anglo-Saxon poetry abounds in poetical phrases, what are known as " kennings," to describe certain recurring experiences of the kind that quicken the imagination, evoke strains of feeling : a ship is " sund-hengest " (sea-horse), and in the same sense " sae-hengest," " waeg-hengest," " yth-mearh," " sae-mearh," or " flod-wudu " and " waegthel " (a wave plank). The sun is " wuldres-gim " (gem of glory) or " godes-candel," and the sword " beada-leoma " (the battle's ray), etc., etc.

Most of these, but not all, disappeared in the centuries when the language of the upper classes was French. With the revival of English poetry in the fourteenth century two fashions contended for a time : the French syllabic metre used with a difference, and the older alliterative form. In both, but especially in the latter, owing to the greater difficulty of the form, one finds a new poetical vocabulary emerging, made up especially of what were called " aureate terms " (in the Low Countries they were called " schuim " or " froth "), words taken over from Latin. So in Chaucer you find " diurnal," " jocounde," " orient," " occident " :

> That al the orient laugheth of the lighte ;

so " Mars armipotent." But on the whole Chaucer's vocabulary is natural and simple and thereby often most effective. Wyld cites :

> What is this world ?   What asketh men to have ?
> Now with his love, now in the colde grave
> Allone, withouten anye companye.

It is in the rhymed and alliterated verse of the poets of the north of England and of Scotland that you find the use and abuse of aureate terms. So in Dunbar you find such a *tour de force* as :

> Hale, sterne superne !   Hale, in eterne
>   In Godes sicht to schyne !
> Lucerne in derne for to discerne
>   By glory and grace devyne ;
> Hodiern, modern, sempitern,
>   Angelical regyne !
> Our tern inferne for to dispern
>   Helpe, rialest rosyne.
> *Ave Maria, gracia plena !*
> Haile, fresche floure femynyne !
> Yerne us, guberne, virgin matern,
>   Of ruth baith rute and ryne . . .

The same kind of thing is seen at its worst, its least poetical, in such work as Hawes' *Passetyme of Pleasure*—" pulchritude," " simplitude," " intellecyon," " facundyous," etc. The ballads of the fifteenth century are of popular adoption if not origin and the language is simple. Yet they have certain recurring epithets and turns :

> And out, and cam the thick, thick bluid,
>   And out and cam the thin ;

> And out and cam the bonny herts bluid ;
>   Thair was nae life left in.

> Says, Christ thee save, thou proud porter ;
> Sayes, Christ thee save and see.

> He hadna ridden a mile, a mile
> A mile but barely three.

Or

> He had never a penny left in his purse,
> Never a penny left but three.

The simplest objects are made of silver and gold :

> By this Lord Barnard was come to the dore.
> And lighted upon a stone ;
> And he pulled out three silver keyes,
> And opened the dores each one.

Of later, post-Renaissance diction the fountain-head is Spenser, as Professor Wyld has pointed out very fully of late. In his poetry the older tradition of romance and allegory combines with the new spirit of humanism, with its high sense of human values, and delight in elaborations and refinements of diction, texture, and metre. He accepted metrically the adaptation of French syllabic metre to the English stress or accent and slurring which Chaucer and the older poets had worked out, not without difficulty. But he did not abandon the English tradition of, and taste for, alliteration, but used as the ear directed, not according to any fixed rule as in Anglo-Saxon. For diction he claimed the whole English language as at his disposal, and with that the right to expand it ; and we shall find in his diction all the devices which Aristotle recounts and which were to be the heritage of English poets—archaisms, provincialisms, coinages, fresh compounds, foreign words, older forms of current words, or forms of his own devising.

But Spenser's departures from current use are, as with every artist, determined by the end he has in view, the kind of effect he wishes to secure. Thus, in the pastorals, with their cult of *simplesse*, a return to nature, he makes free use of provincialisms : " lass," " brickle," " louting low," " sperre the gate," " garre them disagree," etc. The archaisms have much the same effect, for many of them were probably still in use among the peasantry : " yclept," " glitterand," " hugy." You will notice that it is in

G

the satirical attacks on the clergy especially that the provincialisms abound :

> Diggon Davie, I bid her god day :
> Diggon her is, or I missay ?
>
> Diggon was her, while it was daylight,
> But now her is a most wretched wight.

In *The Faerie Queene*, where the poet's aim is to recapture the spirit of mediæval romance, there are fewer provincialisms but more archaisms :

> Yet *mote* he *algates* now abide, and answer make.
>
> The royal maid *wox* inly wonder glad,

and endless other words and forms ; " uneath," " uncouth," " yfere," " to fray," " tort " (wrong). One may say, I think, that the spirit of chivalrous romance is so identified with the Middle Ages that every reviver, from Spenser to Scott and William Morris, has had to archaise to some extent to get the requisite atmosphere. But Spenser was aiming also at the dignity of great poetry, and accordingly you find him, like his Anglo-Saxon predecessors of whom he probably knew nothing, using the kind of elevated metaphorical periphrasis which Aristotle illustrates from Greek poetry. The sun is the " great eye of heaven " ; the sea " the watery wilderness " ; water is " crystalline humour " ; fish are " the finny drove " ; cows " milkie mothers." In this kind of phrasing Spenser was to be followed by many who made no attempt to adopt the archaic manner of his romance. Milton has " fleecy wealth " for sheep ; and speaks of the bees' " straw-built citadel." Dryden speaks of sheep as the " fleecy store," and Pope as the " fleecy breed." There is no harm in such imaginative periphrases if they are effectively used and appropriately. But the tendency was for them to become stereotyped, and it was against this that Wordsworth rebelled, though he himself is capable of " itinerant vehicle " for " stage-coach," and in a good poem he speaks of the body as " this corporeal frame." It was such phrases, and the use of certain fixed epithets which are also largely traceable to Spenser, and of personifications which had no inspiration behind them, that constituted what Wordsworth called

" pseudo-poetic diction " : " verdant mead," " purling brook,"
" gelid cistern " for " cold bath," and personifications such as

> Let Observation with extensive view
> Survey mankind from China to Peru.

Of course the epithets of a great poet are among his most delightful
devices, as Milton's " lucid streams " and " irriguous valley " and
Wordsworth's " pellucid lake " and the " earth's diurnal course."

Spenser's compounds include the " sea-shouldering whales "
already quoted, " leather-winged bats," " heart-binding " and
" heart-robbing eyes." His foreign words include French, as
" selle " for saddle, " corages " for hearts or nature, " retired "
for withdrawn, " oeillades " for glances, and even Spanish,
" bascimano." Latin words are used in their original sense :
" revoke " for " call back " and " edifyed " for " built," etc.
But read for Spenser's diction both Professor Wyld's *Spenser's
Diction and Style in Relation to those of Later English Poetry*
(1930) and his *Some Aspects of the Diction of English Poetry*
(1933).

But though Spenser was to be an influence on the diction of
what, at any rate till lately, has been regarded as the classical
tradition of English poetry—Milton, Dryden, Pope, Thomson,
Gray, Collins, Cowper, Crabbe — and was still an influence with
Wordsworth, Coleridge, Scott and Byron, he did not find any
immediate imitators of the very artificial style of the *Faerie
Queene*. He was the last poet of chivalrous romance after the
mediæval tradition till the revival of the nineteenth century,
except it be Chatterton. Of his diction Jonson declared " Spenser
writ no language," and Jonson himself in his poems, Donne,
and the " Metaphysical " school generally wrote a very pure and
natural English. George Herbert, for example, is the master of
a very pure English which does not prevent him from the use of
bold metaphor, calling the day " the bridal of the earth and sky "
and spring " a box where sweets compacted lie," but these are not
periphrastic means of avoiding the calling of a thing by its usual
name. Nor can the dramatists be called Spenserians, though
Mr Charles Crawford has traced the imitation of Spenser in
certain plays and in Marlowe. But it is not his archaisms
that they attempt to follow. The great characteristic of the style

of the dramatists is their wealth of imagery, metaphor, and all the language which I have called the natural language of emotion, used by those who as poets have a more vivid and transfiguring imagination than most of us. It is not only Shakespeare who might in modern use be called an " imagist." Take a passage at random from Lamb's *Specimens*, and you will see what I mean :

> And why on me ? why should the envious world
> Throw all their scandalous malice upon me ?
> Cause I am poor, deform'd and ignorant,
> And like a bow buckled and bent together
> By some more strong in mischiefs than myself ;
> Must I for that be made a common sink
> For all the filth and rubbish of men's tongues
> To fall and run into ?
>
> (Ford, Dekker, and Rowley, *The Witch of Edmonton.*)

Wordsworth's protest did help to clear away the dead element in the traditional diction, the belief that it was poetic to call " trundling a hoop "

> To chase the rolling circle's speed ;

to call sheep " a fleecy care " ; to turn the prayer " God rest his soul ! " into " Eternal blessings on his shade attend ! "—not to speak of the ever-recurring epithets " breathing spring," " blushing flowers," " crystal spring," etc., etc. Shelley, in the main, uses all the essential language of feeling and poetry—metaphor, personification, etc.—but otherwise the diction of song after song is as pure as that of Herbert. " I have avoided with great care," he writes in the Preface to *The Cenci*, " . . . the introduction of what is commonly called mere poetry. . . . In a dramatic poem the imagery and the passion should interpenetrate one another, the former being reserved simply for the full development and illustration of the latter. Imagination is the immortal God which should assume flesh for the redemption of mortal passion. It is thus that the most remote and the most familiar imagery may alike be fit for dramatic purposes when employed in the illustration of strong feeling which raises what is low, and levels to the apprehension that which is lofty, casting over all the shadows of its own greatness. . . . In other respects I have written more carelessly ; that is without an over-fastidious and learned choice of words. In this respect I entirely agree with those modern critics who assert that in order to move men to true sympathy we must use the familiar language of men. . . . But it must be the real language of men in general and not that of any particular class to whose society the writer happens to belong." So he refers to the controversy which Wordsworth had aroused. But the Spenser of the Romantics was John Keats. The Glossary affixed to the edition of his poems by the late Professor de Selincourt will show how his style abounds in archaisms :

> The owl for all his feathers was *a-cold*,

in coinages :

> And *diamonded* with panes of quaint device,

and words of one class used as if in another :

> The amorous promise of her lone *complain*,

and so on. In Tennyson's poetry something of a new poetic style, as distinct from that of prose as Milton's in another way, emerges with the beauties and the faults of such a mannered diction. One may pass such a periphrasis as

> Or where the kneeling hamlet drains
> The chalice of the grapes of God.

It is more difficult to share Mr Gladstone's admiration of a game-pie poetically described :

> And half-cut-down, a pasty costly made,
> Where quail and pigeon, lark and leveret lay
> Like fossils of the rock, with golden yolks
> Imbedded and injellied.

It was against this tendency to a style " too picked, too spruce, too affected " that poets towards the end of the century began to seek a closer approach to the language of everyday conversation. And remember always it is not a question only of the words and figures used. It is the way in which the whole thing is said that makes you feel this is or is not poetic style. Arnold takes as an

example of the effect we call " style " a passage from Milton
compared with one from Goethe : " Compare this from Milton—

> Nor sometimes forget
> Those other two equal with me in fate,
> So were I equall'd with them in renown,
> Blind Thamyris and blind Maeonides—

with this from Goethe :

> Es bildet ein Talent sich in der Stille,
> Sich ein Charakter in dem Strom der Welt.

(' A talent may be formed in a quiet life. Character in the stream
of the world's life.') Nothing can be better in its way than the
style in which Goethe there presents his thought, but it is the style
of prose as much as of poetry ; it is lucid, harmonious, earnest,
eloquent, but it has not received that peculiar kneading, heightening, and recasting which is observable in the style of the passage
from Milton, a style which seems to have for its cause a certain
pressure of emotion, and an ever surging, yet bridled excitement
in the poet, giving a special intensity to his way of delivering
himself." That is well said, and you will find the same, yet
different, moulding in Shakespeare, in passages approximating
more closely than Milton ever does to the style of prose. But if the
moulding becomes a mannerism, is not supported by the pressure
of emotion, the bridled excitement, then you get the style of too
much in the *Idylls of the King* and Alexander Smith's *Edwin
of Deira*. And finally remember, first and last, that poetry is,
as Dante puts it, *musice composita*. The effect of a poem depends
not only, perhaps not mainly, on the words as conveying sense,
nor as conveying colour by their associations, but on their effect
on the ear and in the mouth (see p. 30). To the fine ear of
Saintsbury, or of a poet like Miss Edith Sitwell, the essential
quality of a poem may be conveyed by the interplay of vowel and
consonant throughout the whole—the alliterations and the rhymes.
(See her delightful *A Poet's Notebook*, Macmillan, 1943).

CHAPTER VI

CONSTRUCTION—THE SENTENCE

Iam vero ea, quae invenerit, quâ diligentia collocabit, quoniam id secundum erat de tribus : vestibula nimirum honesta, aditusque ad causam faciet illustres ; cumque animos prima aggressione occupaverit, confirmabit sua, infirmabit excludetque contraria ; de firmissimis alia prima ponet, alia postrema, inculcabitque leviora.—Cicero : *Orator*, xv. 50.

WORDS are the materials with which we have to work in composition, the bricks of our building, the simplest elements available for the communication by speech of our thoughts and feelings. But " composition " means the " putting together " of words. The significance of an isolated word, not a member of a sentence, is general and abstract—an indication supplied by the dictionary of a thought which the word may be used to convey rather than the symbol of a definite object or idea. The full meaning, colour, and harmony of words depend on their combination with others in sentences ; the sentences themselves on their interaction in the paragraph ; and the paragraph itself is a unit in other, larger divisions—chapter or canto or act—in the whole composition. What we propose to consider next is the sentence and the paragraph, beyond which, Professor Saintsbury declares, consideration of style does not extend. That we shall discuss later.

Here again the determining principles, our guiding stars, are the subject-matter, the purpose, and the audience ; and these we have reduced temporarily to a consideration of the style which we choose to write in and the means by which that particular style is produced and maintained. The colourless precision of a scientific treatise, the plainness of the style which Bishop South commended, the charm of ornate prose and verse, the power of the grand style to transport an audience—all these depend not only on the choice of words but on their arrangement. A scientific style is as clearly indicated by the arrangement of its clauses, the choice of connecting words and phrases, as by its use of an abstract and philosophical terminology. The charm of the plain, homely style lies not more in the racy character of its phraseology than in the native purity of the idiom and the direct natural order of the words. While of the decorative style the effect depends no less on the musical cadence of the words and their combinations than on the picturesque and transfiguring power of word and image.

Correctness of idiom, otherwise grammatical correctness, and the right ordering of the words are then our first concern, the latter to be determined, as we shall see, by more than one consideration. But, to begin with, a word on grammar.

As with propriety in the use of words so with grammatical correctness, the governing principle is good usage. It is not the business of the grammarian to prescribe laws to a language, but to ascertain and define the usages of those who are recognised as speaking the language well. The error of attempting to lay down laws not based on actual usage has been occasionally made by English grammarians, because for a long time they were disposed to think that English grammar should, so far as possible, be accommodated to the grammar of a language which was much more studied than English, namely Latin. As a fact, English grammar and Latin differ from one another in some essential respects.

Latin syntax lays stress on three things : (1) agreement, *e.g.*, of adjective with noun, relative pronoun with antecedent, verb with subject, etc. ; (2) government, *i.e.* the determination of the case of a noun by the word on which it depends; and (3) the distinction between principal and subordinate statement. The indicative is, generally speaking, the mood of the principal statement, the infinitive or subjunctive generally that of dependent, subordinate statement. In modern English, owing mainly to the loss of inflections, all these considerations have become of very little importance. The number of possible agreements in form is very small : adjectives have no terminations ; in the verb only the third person singular has a distinctive termination, and that only in the present tense. The result is that even when such distinctive terminations or forms do exist strict formal agreement is often violated for the sake of the sense.[1] It is the same with regard to

[1] " Here," says a Dutch writer on English grammar, " the English language occupies a unique position among the modern languages. On the one hand, it is quite common, or even usual, for a singular noun with a plural

government. Only the pronouns have different forms for the nominative and the objective, and the order of words frequently leads to disregard of what would be correct government. In subordinate statements there are in English some very idiomatic uses of the infinitive, with or without " to," and of the participle. But the subjunctive is practically unknown to the spoken English of to-day.

A distinctively English idiom is the use of nouns as adjectives expressive both of qualities and of relations : " Russia needs help to foster her *infant* colonies," " Nowhere have these complaints been more just than in the *China* trade." Both these examples are cited from *The Times*. " The attributive use of the common case form of a noun is," writes Poutsma, " a highly interesting feature of the English language, to which there is hardly a parallel in either Dutch or German." Nouns and adjectives are used side by side : " The sepulchre has oped his *ponderous* and *marble* jaws," " *The Review of Reviews* is absolutely independent and is free from any national, sex, class, sectarian and denominational bias." Nevertheless, general as this idiom is, it is apparently felt to be a makeshift, because, when an adjective does exist, we no longer use the noun. We say " Transvaal Government " but " English Government." If the noun is frequently used as an adjective it can so far assume the character of a pure adjective as to be even compared ; *e.g.* Tennyson writes

And I would be the girdle about her dainty waist,

but Shakespeare has

The hand of little employment has the daintier sense,

and we find also " There stood waiting for her the daintiest of little broughams." We are always coining new adjectives. The stylistic consideration is, should we rest content with the noun, or should we coin an adjective, and that not from native but from

meaning to be construed as plural ; on the other hand, we meet with frequent instances of a plural noun denoting a singular idea being dealt with as a singular. Anything of the kind is only occasionally found in French or German or Dutch." (H. Poutsma : *A Grammar of late Modern English for the use of Continental, especially Dutch, Students.* Groningen, 1904, 1914.)

Several Shakespearean concords are thus still admitted in certain cases, *e.g.* " forty yards is a good distance " (Sheridan).

Latin roots ?   The English language abounds in adjectives of Latin origin corresponding to nouns of purely English descent :

mouth	oral	father	paternal
ox	bovine	king	royal, regal
star	stellar	house	domestic.

Many of these are quite unnecessary, but English adjectives have not been coined to take their place because we can use the noun as an adjective. As Jespersen says : " ' birthday ' is much more English than ' natal day,' and ' eye-ball ' than ' ocular globe,' but physiologists think it more dignified to speak of the ' gustatory nerves ' than of ' taste-nerves,' and will even say ' mental nerve ' (Latin *mentum* = a chin) instead of ' chin-nerve ' in spite of the unavoidable confusion with the familiar adjective ' mental.' "

The influence of teachers has been too much in favour of these pedantic coinages. The best rule is to stick to the noun unless (*a*) the meaning is ambiguous, for the different meanings of the compounds of nouns with nouns are very puzzling : " house-boat " and " boat-house," or again " home-farm " and " baby-farm " ; (*b*) there is a good adjective the colour of which suits your style. Consider, for example, such adjectives as " earthen," " hempen," " leathern," " oaken," etc., which have not quite the same effect as would be conveyed simply by the use of the noun.

Of grammar, then, a writer may take as his rules (*a*) that he is justified in adhering to established English idiom despite apparent violation of rules of concord and agreement borrowed from an inflected language [1] such as Latin ; (*b*) that indeed he should

---

[1] A good English idiom which Dryden, after using it freely himself, attempted to reject (an example which others have followed), is the closing of a sentence with a preposition. But the preposition really forms often a portion of the verb and comes quite correctly and idiomatically at the close of a sentence. We form our compounds of verb and preposition not as formerly (and in German and some other languages) by *prefixing* the preposition but by placing it *after* the verb and that without actually attaching it to the verb. We say " to run after," " to come to," " to speak about." In doing so we frequently bring the preposition in a considerable distance after the verb, it may be at the end of a sentence. " Houses are built to live in, not to look on " (Bacon). Dryden, in his earlier writings, used the idiom frequently, for it belongs to a conversational style. Later, probably under the influence of French, he speaks of it as a common fault in the style of Ben Jonson, " and which I have but lately observed in my own writings." He revised the sentences in which he

resist the importation of foreign idioms, Latin, French, etc., unless usage has finally sanctioned them ; (c) that the worst breaches of English grammar are those which involve confusion of thought. Such confusion is not infrequently due to exaggerated consideration of agreement and government, and neglect of the great importance of arrangement.

For the mutual relation of words in an English sentence is shown, not to any large extent by inflection, but by the proximity of words to one another within a certain pattern. I prefer to put it thus, rather than, with some writers on rhetoric, to speak of a " rule of proximity," viz. " things which are to be thought of together must be mentioned as closely as possible together " (Herbert Spencer), because, abstractly considered, proximity might be secured by other arrangements than those which English usage has determined. It seems natural to us to write from left to right, but other peoples have done otherwise. So the adjective is quite as near the noun when it follows as when it precedes. But we so much expect the simple adjective to precede the noun that " a garden flower " is a different thing from a " flower garden." The French in many cases prefer the latter arrangement, and we use it when the adjective is enlarged by some qualifying phrase. We say " a matter too urgent to be put off longer," where a German would probably prefer " a too urgent to be put off longer matter." There is no essential reason why the verb should not precede the subject, or the object the verb, if by proximity or inflection you make the relation obvious.

It is the observance of a customary order which makes intelligible the bearing of words upon one another. English idiom has stereotyped the order of some combinations, has in the case of others settled a normal though not a universally binding order, has left some more or less unsettled, the proper order to be determined by considerations of coherence and emphasis. It is

---

found it when re-issuing his *Essay of Dramatic Poesy*, but the idiom has remained, and we find as good a writer as Cardinal Newman writing : " Vain man would be wise, and he curiously examines the works of nature, as if they were lifeless and senseless, as if he alone had intelligence and they were base inert matter, however curiously contrived at the first. So he goes on, tracing the order of things, giving names to the wonders he meets with, and thinking he understands what he has *given a name to*. At length he forms a theory, and recommends it in writing, and calls himself a philosopher."

the general rule, our general expectation, that the subject will come first in an English sentence, the predicate verb next, and the object, or other adjunct, at the close—the object being generally the most important of these and therefore coming closest to the verb. As a stereotyped, fixed order we may take it (*a*) that the simple adjective precedes the noun, " the brown pony " : to place it after the noun is a Latinism used for poetic effect, " spirits reprobate " (Milton, *P.L.*, i. 697) ; (*b*) that in questions and the expression of a wish the verb generally precedes the subject— " Are you ill ? " " Where are you going ? " " Long live the king ! " If a qualifying or other word is placed for emphasis at the beginning inversion is frequent — " In the beginning was the word," " Never did I see the like," " Among those in the theatre was the author " ; (*c*) that the indirect object precedes the direct, " He gave him his choice " but " He gave the choice to each in turn."

So much do we count on the order as the determining factor that if, for any reason of interrogation, connection, emphasis, we place a pronoun at the beginning of the sentence, we are apt to put it in the nominative case although it is really the object of the following verb : " Who, I exclaimed, can we consult but Miss P— ? " (Thackeray) ; " She, Claudio, that you wronged, look you restore " (Shakespeare, *Measure for Measure*, v, 1, 523) ; " She, men would have to be your mother once, Old Gandolf envied me so fair she was " (Browning, *The Bishop Orders His Tomb*) ; " I am not yet of Percy's mind, the Hotspur of the north ; he that kills me some six or seven dozens Scots " (Shakespeare, *Henry IV*, ii, 4, 97-8) ; " Know ye not me the Titan ? he who made his agony the barrier to your else all-conquering foe ? " (Shelley, *Prometheus Unbound*, Act I). Occasionally, having opened in this way with the pronoun in the nominative, the writer corrects by reintroducing the pronoun in the objective : " He that can discern the loveliness of things we call him poet " (Carlyle). It is this tendency, Jespersen points out, which has changed many impersonal verbs into personal. We do not say as Milton did, " Much better would it like him to be a messenger of gladness."

On the other hand, if the pronoun follows the verb, we are apt to put it in the accusative or objective case. The notorious example is, " It is me," which used to be censured by teachers.

But as Jespersen pointed out, no one would correct Shelley's " Be thou, Spirit fierce, my spirit, be thou *me*, impetuous one ! " (*Ode to the West Wind*). But older writers give bolder instances, as " And damn'd be him that first cries hold, enough ! " The nominative absolute has replaced the older dative because the pronoun precedes the verb : " For he being dead, with him is beauty slain " (Shakespeare). In " fare thee well " " thee " has taken the place of " thou " because it follows the verb. It is in the use of pronouns that these irregularities occcur, the noun having no cases to be rightly or wrongly used. What the errors, as they must be counted from the point of view of an inflected language, show is that the order of the words counts for more in our minds, our feelings, than the thought of government or agreement, which in Latin would be the first considerations. Any such mistakes in a Latin composition would be reckoned " howlers " and so penalised.

For as with government so is it with agreement : English usage is lax, going more by the sense or feeling than by rule. Collective nouns may be used with a singular or a plural verb according as we think of the thing represented as a whole or in its members separately. Jespersen, in his *Essentials of English Grammar* (London, 1933), gives a good example of the two usages in one sentence : " The Garth family, which *was* rather a large one, for Mary had four brothers and one sister, *were* very fond of their old house " (George Eliot). Some groups take a singular verb : " Is twenty thousand kisses such a trouble ? " (Shakespeare), " Fifty yards is counted a good distance." Even when two substantives are connected by " and," if they were felt as constituting a single group older writers often used the singular verb : " Now abideth faith, hope and charity," " renown and grace is dead," " an anomaly and scandal was removed from our legislation." I take these examples from Jespersen, as cited above, who remarks : " By rejecting the singular in such constructions, modern English seems to me to lose in psychological truth what it gains in grammatical uniformity." With " or " and " nor " again we meet with some apparent but defensible departures from the regular singular, as in " John or James was destined to succeed to the living." Sometimes the substantives are really rather added than separated : " Neither I nor my father were ever any good at figures " (Winston Churchill, 13th October 1943) ; " Snuff or the fan supply each pause of chat " (Pope) ; " Neither the morning nor the evening star are so fair " (Coleridge)—that is " both are less fair." Similar variations in the number occur with " none," " any " : " None feels it more than I do," " None are wretched but by their own fault," " Has any of you a pen ? " " Were any of them found guilty ? " The sense is the determining factor. But for all the idiomatic, often queer irregularities of English grammar, one must consult such works as Jespersen's *Growth and Structure of the English Language* ; *A Modern English Grammar on Historical Principles ; Essentials of English Grammar*; E. Kruisinga, *A Grammar of Present-day English* ; Poutsma, *A Grammar of late Modern English for the use of Continental, especially Dutch, Students* (Groningen, 1904-14) ; L. Pearsall Smith, *Words and Idioms*, 1925. The interest of continental grammars is that they notice peculiarities of actual usage which our native grammarians are still somewhat inclined to overlook or to condemn as ungrammatical. Speaking broadly, for a foreigner the chief difficulties in English grammar are in the use of prepositions and in the correct use of certain idiomatic usages. A subtle error which sometimes creeps into a foreigner's English is the use of an idiomatic expression, bordering on slang, where a native would probably not think of using it. In speaking a foreign language it is safer to be a little formal at first. For ourselves, some recurring difficulties are in (1) the use of relative clauses, distinguishing restrictive, defining clauses from those which are co-ordinate, make an additional statement — on this depends the right use or wrong use of " and which " ; (2) the right use of " shall " and " will "—the former originally expressing compulsion (must), the latter wish, determination—now used to express the future but with subtle qualifications due to the original sense. Roughly one may distinguish between simple futurity, " I shall, you will," etc., and the will of the speaker, " I will," " you shall," etc. But politeness, or the view that his own will is equivalent to necessity for the persons addressed, will lead the speaker to express his will in the " future " form, " You will go to your room and stay there." Moreover, in questions you generally use the form which you expect the answer to take—" Shall you be in town to-morrow ? " meaning, " Do your affairs bring you there on that day ? " " Will you come to tea ? " that is, " Are you willing ? " etc. (3) Gerund and participle in "-ing "—" I saw him being hanged " and " I have no objection to his being hanged," etc. (see Jespersen, *Essentials of English Grammar*). There are also nice distinctions in the use of other auxiliaries besides those mentioned, *e.g.* " can " and " may." For natives I would add to the works mentioned above Fowler's *Modern English Usage* (1926).

Our first rule, then, for good composition—the putting together of our words to express our meaning correctly and well—is that the grammatical idioms should be English, not Latin or any other ; and that except for good reasons the order of the words should be also the idiomatic normal order. The first difficulty which presents itself after that, of knowing what is good grammar, and what is the usual order of words, is how we are to deal with those parts of a sentence which usage has left comparatively free, movable as we think best for our purpose. Here our guiding stars are, as has been said, coherence and emphasis. Words which modify each other should come as close to one another as possible. We say " a tall young man " rather than " a young tall man," because " young " qualifies man more intimately than does " tall." It is for the sake of variety, for poetical effect, that Stevenson writes :

> Where the old plain men have rosy faces,
> And the young fair maidens quiet eyes.

Ludicrous breaches of this rule of coherence are frequently instanced in manuals of composition. But, like many breaches or alleged breaches of grammar, they are due either to confusion of thought and carelessness, or they are not errors at all, but due to the superior importance of emphasis. For it is when the claims of emphasis come to be considered that rules of proximity or of the idiomatic order of words may have to give way.

It is not infrequently the *single* adverbs or adverbial phrases which are misplaced, " only," " at least," " wholly." As Blair says, in speaking the emphasis of the voice will show what is intended. It is the reader, who must judge by the eye, that may be misled : " The Romans understood liberty at least as well as we " (Swift) may mean that " liberty is the word emphasised." The context shows that the sentence should run, " The Romans understood liberty, as well at least as we," The context does so often show what the writer means that such misplacements, wrong collocations, are more often irritating than misleading. It is by the context, and what you see and feel to be the writer's drift, that you must judge whether the order can be improved. For example, Blair censures the following sentence from a preacher, " It is folly to pretend to arm ourselves against the accidents of life by heaping up treasures, which nothing can protect us against but the good providence of our Heavenly Father," and alters it to " It is folly to pretend by heaping up treasures to arm ourselves against, etc." But it seems to me that to the preacher the words " to arm ourselves against the accidents of life by heaping up treasures " formed one idea. To put the words " by heaping up treasures " so early in the sentence is to leave them for an instant unrelated. I should prefer to say, " It is folly to pretend to arm ourselves against the accidents of life by heaping up treasures, for (or " when ") nothing can protect us against these but the good providence of our Heavenly Father." It is never quite safe to take a sentence out of its context and pronounce upon its correctness.

The importance of emphasis in speaking is obvious. The stress which we lay on certain words, the varying tone of the voice, declares the meaning of a sentence and the degree of feeling with which it is uttered. The problem for the writer is to indicate just where these stresses ought to fall, how the sentence is to be read mentally. There are some artificial aids to this, as marks of exclamation, printing in italics, the use of capitals, and we shall find that some writers make freer use of these than others. But the best writing does not rely on these, but on the relief given, by the shaping of a sentence, to the more important members. To modulate his emphasis well, almost as much as to choose his words and figures rightly, is the sign-manual of a great writer. Swift has defined a good style as the use of proper words in proper places.

For there are many degrees of emphasis, and the good writer no more wishes to exaggerate than to understate. Like a good speaker, he will not gesticulate when the tone of his voice and the gravity of his thought are sufficient of themselves to indicate the relative importance of what he has to say. Heightened emphasis is like the use of hyperbole, a figure not to be lightly used. What one might call the first degree of emphasis is that which is needed to make explicit what is said, simply to obviate misunderstanding. This is secured by beginning and ending, especially ending, the sentences with the proper words. English idiom has given the opening words of a sentence so generally to the subject that in many cases all we have to be sure of is that we have chosen the right subject of the sentence, the subject which the context requires. But greater freedom is left us in the choice of the closing adjunct, and on this will depend often the meaning and the weight of the sentence. The last words are those which clinch the statement. Take a fairly simple example from the New Testament, the famous chapter on love, or charity : " Though I speak with the tongues of men and of angels, and have not charity, I am become as sounding brass, or a tinkling cymbal. And though I have the gift of prophecy, and understand all mysteries, and all knowledge ; and though I have all faith, so that I could remove mountains, and have not charity, I am nothing. And though I bestow all my goods to feed the poor, and though I give my body to be burned, and have not charity, it profiteth me nothing." This is a fairly common type of construction in which the subordinate clauses lead up to the principal statement at the close ; and it is known as the period. In the last two sentences the sense is held up till two or three qualifying clauses have been introduced. The suspense may of course be prolonged much further. Consider the second sentence in the extract from the book by Merz (p. 40) : " Thomson was the first who, in adopting (after much hesitation) the mechanical view of the phenomena of heat, the doctrine of the convertibility and equivalence of the different forms of energy, recognised that, in order to describe natural phenomena correctly, this view required a qualification." In the sentences from St Paul (for the English here follows the Greek order exactly) the motive for the suspension is emotional, to lay passionate stress on the all-importance of charity (or love, as the Revised Version translates the Greek *agape*). In Merz's sentence the motive is the desire to be precise, to be sure that before the main statement comes it has been so qualified as not to be misleading. In either case the important thing is to be sure that the final statement is important enough to justify the suspense, all the qualification. It was from Latin prose, especially the prose of Cicero, and through Latin from the Greek orators and such a

H

master of Greek prose as Plato, that the periodic construction passed to us at the Renaissance. It took some effort to master it. Chaucer, for example, to go a little farther back, introduces the *Canterbury Tales* with an excellent period :

> When that Aprile with his shoures soote
> The droghte of Marche hath perced to the rote,

and so on till only in the twelfth line do you reach the main statement, the principal clause :

> Then longen folk to gon on pilgrimages   etc.

Yet the same writer has the greatest difficulty in translating the Latin periods in his version of the *De Consolatione Philosophiæ* : " Thou seidest eek, by the mouth of the same Plato, that it was a necessarie cause wyse men to taken and desire the governance of comune thinges, for that the governements of citees, y-left in the handes of felonous tormentours citizenes ne sholde nat bringe in pestilence and destruccioun to gode folk." It was in the seventeenth century, in the sermons and other work of preachers and divines that the Ciceronian period, the long complex sentence (not always periodic in the narrower sense of suspending the main predicate to the end) was cultivated, though in the work of some writers there is seen a move away from Cicero in the direction of a more Tacitean, condensed style. As rhetoricians, leaving the religious values of their sermons for other judges, the two greatest preachers were John Donne and Jeremy Taylor. The former, as the more passionate, is the more apt to utilise the effect of suspense : " The soul that is accustomed to direct herself to God upon every occasion ; that as a flower at sunrising conceives a sense of God in every beam of his, and spreads and dilates itself towards him in a thankfulness in every small blessing that he sheds upon her ; that soul that as a flower at the sun's declining contracts, and gathers in, and shuts up herself, as though she had received a blow, whensoever she hears her Saviour wounded by an oath, or blasphemy, or execration ; that soul who, whatsoever string be strucken in her, base or treble, her high or low estate, is ever tuned towards God, that soul prays sometimes when it does not know that it prays." There are some writers, for example Charles Reade, who to secure the full emphasis would have printed the last words in capitals : " THAT SOUL PRAYS SOMETIMES WHEN IT DOES NOT KNOW THAT IT PRAYS." Jeremy Taylor's use of the period is rather different. It is not the emphasis which he is concerned about. What he loves is the flow of clause after clause. See the passage in the *Sermon on the Return of Prayers* beginning, " So have I seen a lark rise from his bed of grass, etc.," which, I fear, South had in view in his remarks quoted earlier on the plain style (pp. 44-5).

But it is the combination of the simplest, most idiomatic and coherent order with the right distribution of emphasis which gives at once the purest and clearest English style. Instead of examining sentences detached from their context, we shall look at some passages which illustrate different degrees in the fusion of natural, idiomatic order and right emphasis, taking our examples from classical English writers, prose-writers in the main. Such passages will show, I think, (*a*) the great normal importance of the end of the sentence ; (*b*) that by various devices the beginning of a sentence can also be made to heighten the emphasis without any striking departure from the idiomatic order of the words ; (*c*) that as the emphasis rises the writer's style will tend to depart from the idiomatic order of words. The unusual order of the sentence, like the use of a figure, *e.g.* personification, is itself an indication of more impassioned utterance.

In a great deal, then, of good prose there is no heightening of the emphasis to attract attention. Over-emphasis can, as in Macaulay and Carlyle, become fatiguing. It is enough to make sure that you have got, keeping the whole paragraph in view, the right subject, and that the sentence ends with the main predicate or some important qualifying clause, which at any rate does not weaken the effect of what has been said. Of classical prose-writers Addison was probably the most studious to avoid anything like undue emphasis. His ideal of prose was that of Dryden—a heightened reflection of good, cultured conversation, free at once of pedantry and of vulgarity. But whereas Dryden wrote primarily for men, and his prose has vigour and weight as well as ease and naturalness, Addison had what he called " the fair sex " in view, and his aim was to write as one might talk to a lady with no undue raising of the voice, no violence of gesticulation, with a graceful carelessness in which art disguises art—a natural, easy, even negligent order attuned, however, to a pleasing rhythm. His emphasis is, like his grammar, generally but by no means always, correct. But it is seldom that a sentence is too obviously pointed. There is often a point, a satirical point, but it is subtly and cleverly disguised, sometimes in what has the appearance of a compliment. (Steele is more chivalrous in his attitude to woman.) Note where the emphasis falls in the following sentences and some of their peculiarities. But before coming to Addison, let me take a short paragraph in which there is no such conscious artifice, no aiming at special emphasis in this or that sentence, because the whole has weight : " If the present war or its causes happen to be the subject of conversation, he lays all the blame upon them (the enemy) alone, and can see neither avarice nor injustice in the planters of our side. If peace be the topic, his counsel is for war ; nor can he think any terms honourable or advantageous that do not put us in possession, not only of all we have conquered, but almost all the enemy have to lose. Thus while our soldiers earn victory abroad, Jack enjoys the price of it at home, and unacquainted with the perils they endure, seems unmindful how long they undergo them. War gives him no uneasiness ; he sits and soaks in profound security ; the distresses, the calamities of mankind neither interrupt his tranquillity nor lessen his draught ; the miseries of his fellow-creatures, like the pictures of a battle, serve rather to excite pleasure than pain. Ten thousand fallen on one field make a curious article in the gazette. Hundreds sunk to the bottom by one broadside furnish out the topic of the day, and zest his coffee : the very tempest guides him to his harbour. In short, he fancies he shows his loyalty by reproaches, and his courage by continuing the war." Could anything so true and weighty be said without the gesticulation of Carlyle or Ruskin or the savage irony of Swift in his similar description of war to the king of the Brobdingnagians ? In not one sentence is there any departure from a normal order. Now turn from Goldsmith to the elegant satire of Addison : " Some months ago my friend Sir Roger, being in the country, enclosed a letter to me, directed to a certain lady, whom I shall here call by the name of Leonora, and as it contained matters of consequence, desired me to deliver it to her with my own hand. Accordingly I waited upon her lady-ship pretty early in the morning, and was desired by her woman to walk into her lady's library, till such time as she was in readiness to receive me. The very sound of a lady's library gave me a great curiosity to see it ; and, as it was some time before the lady came to me, I had an opportunity of turning over a great many of her books, which were ranged together in a very beautiful order. At the end of the folios (which were finely bound and gilt) were great jars of china placed one above another in a very noble piece of architecture. The quartos were separated from the octavos by a pile of smaller vessels which rose in a delightful pyramid. The octavos were bounded by tea-dishes of all shapes and colours, and sizes, which were so disposed on a wooden frame, that they looked like one continued pillar indented with the finest strokes of sculpture and stained with the greatest variety of dyes. That part of the library which was designed for the reception of plays and pamphlets and other loose papers, was enclosed in a kind of square, consisting of one of the prettiest grotesque works that I ever saw, and made up of scaramouches, lions, monkeys, mandarines, trees, shells, and a thousand other odd figures in china-ware. In the midst of the room was a little Japan table, with a quire of gilt paper upon it, and on the paper a silver snuff-box made in the shape of a little book. I found there were several other counterfeit books upon the upper shelves, which were carved in wood, and served only to fill up the number, like faggots in the muster of a regiment. I was wonderfully pleased with such a mixed kind of furniture as seemed very suitable both to the lady and the scholar, and did not know at first whether I should fancy myself in a grotto or in a library."

That is a little jewel of Addisonian prose. There is a slightly periodic character about the first sentence. Otherwise, the order of words in each sentence is simple and idiomatic. Nor is there apparently any attempt to give an emphatic close to each sentence. In the first, " with my own hand " ends the sentence well because it gives the reason of his visit. But " till such time as she was in readiness to receive me," " which were ranged together in a very beautiful order," " in a very noble piece of architecture," " which rose in a delightful pyramid," etc.—none of these *seem* very weighty statements, but they are, in fact, fine strokes of Addisonian irony. The end of each sentence *is* emphatic ; and the emphasis thus thrown on trifling and apparently irrelevant details contributes delicately and penetratingly to what is intended to be the pervading innuendo of the whole paragraph and essay—that Leonora is more interested in the elegant accessories of her books than in their contents.

Addison is not so happy when he undertakes to write on speculative topics. His aim was to bring philosophy down into the market-place ; and the simplicity and elegance of his style undoubtedly helped to interest ordinary readers in serious, intellectual topics. But the tenuity and vagueness of his thought is reflected in the diffuseness of his style, the loose connection between his paragraphs, the occasional errors in his grammar, and the unemphatic endings of sentences which, if they do not actually obscure the sense, weaken the effect. A characteristic Addisonian ending appears in such a sentence as this : " Milton has thus represented the fallen angels reasoning together in a kind of respite from their torments, and creating to themselves a new disquiet amidst their very amusements ; he could not properly have described the sports of condemned spirits without that cast of horror and melancholy he has so judiciously mingled with them." The last clause obviously relaxes the tone of the whole sentence which would have been better preserved by ending on the words : " without a judicious admixture of horror and melancholy."

In the same essay occurs the following : " On this occasion the philosopher rises into that celebrated sentiment, that there is not on earth a spectacle more worthy the regard of a Creator intent on his works than a brave man superior to his sufferings ; to which he adds, that it must be a pleasure to Jupiter himself to look down from Heaven and see Cato amidst the ruins of his country preserving his integrity." Idiomatic order, parallelism, and emphasis would all, I think, have gained by a change of the order : " Cato preserving his integrity amidst the ruins of his country."

The prose of Swift is of the same conversational character as Addison's, and occasionally one meets similar careless endings, *e.g.* " as I before observed," etc. But Swift, like Dryden, is a more masculine writer than Addison ; and generally, without departing from the natural, idiomatic order, he weights and points his sentences with emphatic endings, tips their tails at times with a satirical sting as poisonous as a scorpion's : " I began my discourse by informing his Majesty that our Dominion consisted of two islands, which comprised three mighty kingdoms, under one sovereign, besides our plantations in America. I dwelt long upon the fertility of the soil, and the temperature of our climate. I then spoke at large upon the constitution of an English parliament, partly made up of an illustrious body called the House of Peers ; persons of the noblest blood, and of the most ancient and ample patrimonies. I described the extraordinary care always taken of their education in arts and arms, to qualify them to being counsellors born for the King and Kingdom ; to have a share in the legislation, to be members of the highest courts of judicature, from whence there could be no appeal ; and to be champions always ready for the defence of their Prince and country by their valour, conduct and fidelity. That these were the ornaments and bulwarks of the Kingdom, the followers of their most renowned ancestors, whose honour had been the reward of their virtue, from which their posterity was never once known to degenerate. To these were joined several holy persons, as part of that assembly, under the title of Bishops, whose peculiar business it is to take care of religion and of those who instruct the people therein. These were searched and sought out through the whole nation by the prince and his wisest councillors, among such of the priesthood as were most deservingly distinguished by the sanctity of their lives, and the depth of their erudition ; who were indeed the spiritual fathers of the clergy and the people." Every clause and sentence in this ironical paragraph has its weight and point, yet there is none of the distortions of a similar passage in such an author as Carlyle. In the first sentence there is the same device as we noted in Addison, apparent negligence where the intention is to be emphatic. He flings in " besides our plantations in America " after the weightier " three mighty kingdoms," as much as to say, " I must not forget our precious plantations." The effect would be lost by reading " which comprise, besides plantations in America, three mighty kingdoms, etc.," though that would be normally the more correct arrangement. Thereafter each clause ends strongly. Note the order in " ancient and ample," " from whence there could be no appeal," " valour, conduct and fidelity," " never once known to degenerate," " who were indeed the spiritual fathers of the clergy and the people."

One of the principal charms of such conversational prose as that of Dryden, Swift, or Addison is that the emphasis is never too obtrusive. Queen Victoria complained that Mr Gladstone spoke to her as if she were a public meeting. The natural, easy order of the words is as essential a feature of a conversational prose as colloquial diction and idiom. A more strongly marked emphasis is an indication of a more oratorical style. An excellent example is the prose of Lord Macaulay, a prose that without distortion of the idiomatic order is always emphatic, at times even fatiguingly emphatic. The didactic clearness of his style derives in large measure from the sureness with which the emphasis falls on the important words, important in the sentence or as connectives with the preceding sentence. Consider the following short para- graph : " It is to be regretted that the prose-writings of Milton should, in our time, be so little read. As compositions, they deserve the attention of every man who wishes to become acquainted with the full power of the English language. They abound with passages compared with which the finest declamations of Burke sink into insignificance. They are a perfect field of cloth of gold. The style is stiff with gorgeous embroidery. Not even in the earlier books of *Paradise Lost* has the great poet ever risen higher than in those parts of his controversial works in which his feelings, excited by conflict, find a vent in bursts of devotional and lyrical rapture. It is, to borrow his own majestic language, ' a sevenfold chorus of hallelujahs and harping symphonies.' " This is from an early essay, and Macaulay later somewhat toned down his exuber- ance ; but examine the famous second paragraph in the essay on Ranke's *History of the Popes*, the paragraph on the Roman Catholic Church. Many things help to mark the emphatic state- ments—suspense, antithesis, hyperbole ; but the sentence structure is the main factor. There is no violent distortion of the normal order of words, but the opening and the close of almost every sentence strikes the ear like a drum.

Emphasis in Macaulay's prose is mainly a help to clear exposition, to driving home his dogmatic statements. The emo- tional range of his style is not great. All his devices suggest a loud, peremptory utterance—short, quick sentences, emphatic openings and endings, balance and suspense. It is when we come to writers who aim at more emotional effects that we find a subtler management of emphasis as well as of diction, and that a sharper conflict arises between a normal and an emphatic order of words. Emphatic positions, repetitions, and occasional exclamations are among the principal devices of a prose-writer. It is in the poets that one finds most frequently distortion of the normal order for the sake of emotional effect, of strong emphasis. " O Lord, how manifold are thy works ! in wisdom hast thou made them all : the earth is full of thy riches. So is this great and wide sea, wherein are things creeping innumerable, both small and great beasts. There go the ships : there is that leviathan, whom thou hast made to take his pastime therein."

> Flashed all their sabres bare,
> Flashed as they turned in the air.

> Comes a vapour from the margin, blackening over heath and holt,
> Cramming all the blast before it, in its breast a thunderbolt.

The more normal way of transposing the subject and predicate is by the use of " There is," etc., or " It is " : *e.g.* " It is the choice of the moment which renders a measure serviceable or useless, noxious or salutary." " Now there is in the gallant country of the Universe a fair and delicate town, a corporation called Mansoul."

The prose-writer who has gone farthest in the pursuit of emphasis by every available means is Carlyle. It was the late Sir Walter Raleigh who described his prose as resembling an epileptic fit. Witticisms are never quite true. Carlyle's distortion of order, exclamations, dropping of predicate, apostrophes, produce an effect at once clear to explicitness, emphasis, emotional accompaniment, humour and tragedy. Take an example at random : " So wags and wavers this unrestful world, day after day, month after month. The streets of Paris, and all cities, roll daily their oscillatory flood of men ; which flood does nightly disappear, and lie hidden horizontal in beds and truckle-beds ; and awakes on the morrow to new perpendicularity and movement. Men go their roads, foolish or wise :—Engineer Goguelat to and fro, bearing Queen's cipher. A Madame de Stael is busy ; cannot clutch her Narbonne from the Time-flood ; a Princess de Lamballe is busy ; cannot help her Queen. Barnave, seeing the Feuillants dispersed, and Coblentz so brisk begs by way of final recompense to kiss her Majesty's hand ; augurs not well of her new course ; and retires home to Grenoble, to wed an heiress there. The Café Valois and Meot the Restaurateur's hear daily gasconnades ; loud babble of Half-Pay Royalists with or without poniards. . . . But Social Explosions have in them something dread, and as it were magical ; which indeed Life always secretly has : thus the dumb Earth (says Fable) if you pull her mandrake-roots, will give a dæmonic mad-making *moan*. These explosions and Revolts ripen, break forth like dumb dread Forces of Nature ; and they are yet Men's forces ; and we are part of them ; the Dæmonic that is in man's life has burst out on us, will sweep us away too ! —One day here is like another, and yet it is not like but different. How much is growing, silently resistless, at all moments ! Thoughts are growing : forms of Speech are growing, and Customs and even Costumes ; still more visibly are actions and transactions growing, and that doomed Strife of France with herself and with the whole world." Capitals, italics, ellipses, inversions, figures—everything is combined to sustain the effect of an exciting crisis in history described and commented on. It is not a style to be lightly imitated.

The importance of the close, the end, for giving the right emphasis naturally and without undue distortion is further illustrated by its importance for the rhythm of a sentence. Rhythmical prose goes back through Cicero to the Greek orators and to Gorgias, as was pointed out earlier. But in all prose that is prose there will be found an element of rhythm, namely balance. His ear warns a writer or speaker to avoid combining a very long with a very short clause, if it can be avoided. A certain type of sentence was known to the teachers of rhetoric as the balanced sentence. In this not only are the clauses or phrases of much the same length, but they are similarly constructed : " It is easy to laugh at the folly of him who refuses immediate ease for distant pleasure, and instead of enjoying the blessings of life, lets life glide away in preparations to enjoy them ; it affords such opportunities of triumphant exultation to exemplify the uncertainty of the human state, to rouse mortals from their dream, and inform them of the silent celerity of time, that we may believe authors willing rather to transmit than examine so advantageous a principle, and more inclined to pursue a track so smooth and so flowery, than attentively to consider whether it leads to truth." (Johnson, *The Rambler*, quoted in Minto's *Manual of English Prose Literature* as containing " five different balances.")

It was Thrasimachus, Cicero tells us, who deliberately introduced metrical cadences into prose for rhetorical effect, though of course others had done so unpremeditatedly. " The pleasing result was noticed and *certi cursus conclusionesque verborum* (*Orat.* 178) now became a part of rhetorical technique." [1] The view of ancient writers on prose rhythm was that it was most noticeable in the cadence or close of the clause or the period. Study has revealed that there were certain recognised *cursus* or closing rhythms. In classical prose the rhythms were determined by the length of the syllables, but as accentual pronunciation took the place of that by quantity, these continued and were, *e.g.*, " in the eleventh and twelfth centuries adopted by the Roman Curia and rules for it laid down by various Popes " (Clark, *op. cit.*). Some of these have been frequently used, deliberately or not, and recent writers have inquired whether there are not other closing rhythms peculiar to English. I do not propose to go into the subject at length here, but have touched on it to emphasise the doctrine I have preached of the importance of the close of the sentence.

One rhythm to be avoided is that of blank verse in prose. Dickens is rather given to this cadence, but he has some effective closing cadences : " The doctor gently brushed the scattered ringlets of the child from the face and the mouth of the mother. Alas ! how calm they lay there ; how little breath there was to stir them ! Thus clinging fast to that slight spar within her arms the mother drifted out upon the dark and unknown sea that rolls round all the world." The last eleven words compose an Alexandrine. Our greatest conscious cultivators of prose rhythms are Hooker, the great preachers, notably Donne (see the sentence at p. 104), Jeremy Taylor, Milton, Addison, Burke, Johnson, De Quincey, Ruskin. One of the very finest seems to me a sentence

---

[1] *The Cursus in Mediæval and Vulgar Latin*, by Albert C. Clark, M.A., Oxford : at the Clarendon Press, 1910. See also the same writer's *Prose Rhythm in English* : at the Clarendon Press, 1913. The latter lecture was evoked by Saintsbury's *History of English Prose Rhythm* : London, 1912. See also an essay by Oliver Elton, " English Prose Numbers," in *Essays and Studies by Members of the English Association*, iv, 1913.

in Milton, a *cursus* which does not, I think, come under any of the classical heads : " Come forth out of thy royal chamber, O Prince of all the Kings of the earth, put on the visible robes of thy imperial sceptre which thy Almighty Father hath bequeathed thee ; for now thy Bride calls thee, and all creatures sigh to be renewed." Burke has more magnificent, if more rhetorical than poetical, cadences : " With all the impetuosity of youth and all the avarice of age they pour in, wave after wave, and there is nothing before the eyes of the Indians but an endless, hopeless prospect of fresh flights of birds of prey and passage with appetite continually renewing for a prey that is continuing wasting." " Their prey is lodged in England and the cries of the Indians are given to the winds and seas to be blown about at every breaking up of the monsoon over a remote and unhearing ocean." But such elaborate rhythms are for an elevated style. Study rather the simpler cadences of the Bible or the Collects in the prayer-book. Make sense and right emphasis the end you have in view when shaping your sentence, but try also, if you can, at least to avoid harsh concatenations of consonants and unrhythmical successions of stressed and unstressed syllables. Trust to, but train your ear.

CHAPTER VII

CONSTRUCTION—THE PARAGRAPH

A collection, or series, of sentences with unity of purpose.—Bain.

The two capital secrets of prose are these : first, the philosophy of transition and connexion, or the art by which one step in the evolution of thoughts is made to arise out of another : all fluent and effective composition depends on the connexions ; secondly, the way in which sentences are made to modify each other ; for the most powerful effects in written eloquence arise out of this reverberation, as it were, from each other in a rapid succession of sentences ; and because some limitation is necessary to the length and complexity of sentences, in order to make the interdependence felt. Hence it is that the Germans have no eloquence. The construction of German prose tends to such immoderate length of sentences that no effect of intermodification can ever be apparent. Each sentence stuffed with innumerable clauses of restriction and other parenthetical circumstances becomes a separable section, an independent whole.—De Quincey.

It has always been my practice to cast a long paragraph in a single mould, to try it by my ear, to deposit it in my memory, but to suspend the action of the pen till I had given the last polish to my work.—Gibbon.

The ideal paragraph is, as De Quincey's description well suggests, an expanded sentence, a number of consecutive sentences bearing on one subject. For such an ideal paragraph Dr Bain, in the first version of his *English Composition and Rhetoric* (1866), gives some rules which one may keep in mind as a desirable goal to aim at. (1) The bearing of each sentence upon what precedes should be explicit and unmistakable. (2) When several sentences iterate or illustrate the same idea they should as far as possible be formed alike. This in the paragraph corresponds to the balanced sentence described above. Bain calls it the rule of parallel construction. But it is a rule to be observed with caution and consideration of the effect on the mind and the ear. (3) The opening sentence, unless so constructed as to be obviously preparatory, is expected to indicate with prominence the subject of the paragraph. (4) As in the sentence, so in the paragraph, a due proportion should obtain between principal and subordinate statement. These are the four most important rules, or counsels of perfection. Two others, requiring unity and forbidding dislocation, come really under the definition of a paragraph. One may take the sonnet as a good example of a paragraph, if it is not as it can be a single long sentence :

> Let me not to the marriage of true minds
> Admit impediments. Love is not love
> Which alters when it alteration finds,
> Or bends with the remover to remove :
> Oh, no ! it is an ever-fixed mark
> That looks on tempests, and is never shaken ;
> It is the star to every wandering bark,
> Whose worth's unknown, although his height be taken.
> Love's not Time's fool, though rosy lips and cheeks
> Within his bending sickle's compass come ;
> Love alters not with his brief hours and weeks,
> But bears it out even to the edge of doom.
>> If this be error, and upon me proved,
>> I never writ, nor no man ever loved.

This is poetry, and like much poetry it is iterative. The same thing is said once and again to give it all the emphasis which the writer's feelings demand. Such iteration is not unknown in prose also, as we shall see. But on the other hand the sonnet, or prose paragraph, may not thus iterate a statement, but may consist of a closely wrought bit of reasoning :

> If faithful souls be alike glorifi'd
> As Angels, then my father's soul doth see,
> And adds this even to full felicity,
> That valiantly I Hell's wide mouth o'erstride :
> But if our minds be these souls be descried
> By circumstances, and by signs that be
> Apparent in us, not immediately,
> How shall my mind's white truth by them be tried ?
> [For] They see idolatrous lovers weep and mourn,
> And vile blasphemous Conjurers to call
> On Jesus' name, and Pharisaical
> Dissemblers feign devotion. Then turn,
>> O pensive soul, to God, for He knows best
>> Thy true grief, for He put it in my breast.

This is quite a subtle piece of reasoning. " If the souls of the departed see what is going on in our minds as directly as the angels can, then my father will see how valiantly I strive to earn heaven. But if they are, like us, able only to judge by outward signs, how are they to distinguish real grief for sin from fraudulent penitents or devout pharisees, pretenders ? Turn to God to whose grace it is due that this saving sorrow is in your heart ! He cannot fail to see what He himself put there." Note the connecting words, " If . . . then," " But if . . . how," " Then." In a prose paragraph you could, to be explicit, place " For " before line 9, " They see, etc." Now compare this with a prose paragraph from Arnold, who carries the explicit linking of the arguments almost to excess : " *But* after the Restoration the time had come when our nation felt the imperious need of a fit prose. *So also* the time had *likewise* come when our nation felt the *imperious need* of freeing itself from the absorbing preoccupation which religion in the Puritan age had exercised. It was impossible that *this freedom* should be brought about without some negative excess, without some neglect and impairment of the religious life of the soul ; and the spiritual history of the eighteenth century shows us that *the freedom* was not achieved without *them*. *Still the freedom was achieved* ; the preoccupation, an undoubtedly baneful and retarding one if it had continued, was got rid of. *And as with religion amongst us at that period, so it was with letters*. A fit prose was a necessity ; *but* it was impossible that *a fit prose* should establish itself amongst us without some touch of frost to *the imaginative life of the soul*. The needful qualities for *a fit prose* are regularity, uniformity, precision, balance. The men of letters, whose destiny it may be to bring their nation to the attainment of *a fit prose*, must of necessity, whether they work in prose or verse, give a predominating, an almost exclusive attention to the qualities of *regularity, uniformity, precision, balance*. But *an almost exclusive attention to these qualities* involves some repression and silencing of poetry." I have marked the connecting words throughout. One whole sentence serves as a connective. Others are words and phrases repeated. One gets the feeling of being in a rather dull class at school which has to have everything made clear and explicit. But allowing for that, it is a good expository paragraph. Exposition is not the same as argument. It resembles rather description : not description of a scene but of a state of affairs— the constitution of a country, the political condition of, say,

Europe after or before a war. Of objective description or exposition I have given a good example in Merz's passage on p. 40, his account of the steps in the formulation of a theory in physics. Of one in which both objective facts and subjective reactions to these facts combine let me take one from Gibbon, a very careful paragrapher as my quotation above shows; it is that in which he adumbrates the considerations which may have led Constantine to accept Christianity as the State religion : " The counsels of princes are more frequently influenced by views of temporal advantage than by consideration of abstract and speculative truth. The partial and increasing favour of Constantine may naturally be referred to the esteem which he entertained for the moral character of the Christians, and to a persuasion that the propagation of the Gospel would inculcate the practice of private and public virtue. Whatever latitude the absolute monarch may assume in his own conduct, whatever indulgence he may claim for his own passions, it is undoubtedly his interest that all his subjects should respect the natural and civil obligations of society. But the operation of the wisest laws is imperfect and precarious. They seldom inspire virtue, they cannot always restrain vice. Their power is insufficient to prohibit all that they condemn, nor can they always punish the actions which they prohibit. The legislators of antiquity had summoned to their aid the powers of education and of opinion. But every principle which had once maintained the vigour and purity of Rome and Sparta was long since extinguished in a declining and despotic empire. Philosophy still exercised her temperate sway over the human mind, but the cause of virtue derived very feeble support from the influence of the Pagan superstition. Under these discouraging circumstances, a prudent magistrate might observe with pleasure the progress of a religion which diffused among the people a pure, benevolent, and universal system of ethics, adapted to every duty and every condition of life ; recommended as the will and reason of the Supreme Deity, and enforced by the sanction of eternal rewards and punishments. The experience of Greek and Roman history could not inform the world how far the system of national manners might be reformed and improved by the precepts of a divine revelation ; and Constantine might listen with some confidence to the flattering and indeed reasonable assurances of Lactantius.

The eloquent apologist seemed firmly to expect, and almost ventured to promise, *that* the establishment of Christianity would restore the innocence and felicity of the primitive age ; *that* the worship of the true God would extinguish war and dissension among those who mutually considered themselves as the children of a common parent ; *that* every impure desire, every angry or selfish passion, would be restrained by the knowledge of the Gospel ; and *that* the magistrate might sheathe the sword of justice among a people who would be universally actuated by the sentiments of truth and piety, of equity and moderation, of harmony and universal love " (Gibbon, *Decline and Fall of the Roman Empire*, ch. xx). A similar paragraph follows on the doctrine of passive obedience, " which must have appeared in the eyes of an absolute monarch the most conspicuous and useful of the evangelic virtues."

Compare with these an argumentative paragraph : " To limit the expression of opinion in war-time to opinion which does not hinder its prosecution is in fact to give the executive an entirely free hand, whatever its policy, and to assume that, while the armies are in the field, an absolute suspension of criticism is imperative. That is surely a quite impossible position. No one, who has watched at all carefully the process of government in time of war, can doubt that criticism was never more necessary. Its limitation is, in fact, an assurance that mistakes will be made. For, once the right to criticise is withdrawn, the executive commits all the natural follies of dictatorship. It assumes a semi-divine character for its acts. It deprives the people of information essential to a proper judgment of its policy. It misrepresents the situation it confronts by that art of propaganda which enables it to deceive its friends without deceiving its enemies. A people in war-time is always blind to the facts of its position and anxious to believe only agreeable news ; the government takes care to provide it only with news that is pleasant. If no news of such a kind is at hand it will be manufactured. Petty successes will be magnified into resounding victories ; defeats will be minimised wherever possible. The agony of the troops will be obscured by the clouds of censorship. A war-time government is always obtuse to suggestion, angry when inquiry is suggested, careless of truth. It can, in fact, only be moralised to the degree to which it is subjected to critical examination in every aspect of its policy. And to penalise, therefore, the critic is not only to poison the moral foundations of the state, but to make it extremely difficult, when peace comes, for both government and the mass of citizens to resume the habits of normal decency." (H. J. Laski.)

The opening sentence of the first of these two paragraphs is the statement of what the writer takes to be a general truth, of which Constantine's action will prove to be a particular example. It introduces, that is, a paragraph intended to emphasise, with a touch of irony, the temporal advantages as opposed to the strictly religious advantages which weighed with a monarch. Note for yourself the connecting links throughout—conjunctions, pronouns, phrases such as "under these discouraging circumstances." In the next paragraph the opening sentence states the position which the writer will refute, as the second sentence makes obvious, "That is surely a quite impossible position."

It is in expository writing that the careful construction of the paragraph is very important. That is why I have suggested the sonnet as a model, a poetic form in which unity has always been emphasised. For in narrative one has to be content with what falls a good deal short of such an ideal paragraph, to be content with bringing together sentences that are more closely connected with each other than with what precedes or follows. It will be possible to divide into longer or shorter paragraphs according to one's probable readers, their ability to follow a continuous flow without breaks to reconsider. And not only the reader but the subject, remembering what was said in my second chapter of the determining factors— reader, subject, and purpose. In simple narrative you no more want elaborate paragraphs than sentences. What Gibbon says of his paragraph-construction is quite in keeping with the effect on the mind and ear of his great "bridge between the ancient world and the modern," as Carlyle called the *Decline and Fall*. But there is charm also in the simplicity of early prose with its often endless paragraphs and simply linked sentences : " And Jacob went out from Beer-sheba, and went toward Haran. And he lighted upon a certain place, and tarried there all night, because the sun was set ; and he took of the stones of that place, and put them for his pillows, and lay down in that place to sleep. And he dreamed, and behold a ladder set up on the earth, and the top of it reached to heaven : and behold the angels of God ascending and descending on it. And, behold, the Lord stood above it, and said, I am the Lord God of Abraham thy father, and the God of Isaac : the land whereon thou liest, to thee will I give it, and to thy seed ; and thy seed shall be as the dust of the earth, and thou shalt spread abroad to the west, and to the east, and to the north, and to the south : and in thee and in thy seed shall all the families of the earth be blessed. And, behold, I am with thee, and will keep thee in all places whither thou goest, and will bring thee again into this land ; for I will not leave thee, until I have done that which I have spoken to thee of." The Authorised Version begins a new paragraph with the next words, " And Jacob awaked out of his sleep, etc.," but the Revised Version runs on to the end of the chapter, and either will do. The writer had no paragraphs in view. You will find the same artless yet delightful flow-on in the *Morte D'Arthur* : " Then kyng arthur lete sende for al the children born on may day begoten of lordes and born of ladyes for Merlyn told kynge Arthur he that shold destroye hym shold be borne in that day therefore he sent for them all upon payn of deth and so ther were founde many lordes sones and all were sente unto the kynge and soo was Mordred sente by kyng Lotts wyf and all were put in a ship to the sea and some were four wekes old and some lasse, And so by fortune the shyp drove unto a castel and was al to ryven and destroyed the most part sauf that Mordred was cast up and a good man fonde hym and nourished hym til he was xiiii yere olde and thenne he broghte hym to the Court as it reherceth afterward toward the ende of the deth of Arthur So many lordes and barons of this reame were displeaced for her children were so lost and many put the wyte on Merlyn more than on Arthur so what for drede and what for love they helde their pees But whanne the messager came to kynge Ryons thenne was he woode oute of mesure and purveyed hym for a grete hoost as it rehercyth after in the book of Balyn le saueage that foloweth next after how by adventure Balyn gat the swerd. . . ." It would be affectation to write in that manner now, but I confess to preferring these long loose sentences to the very clipped short sentences in which Macaulay and Bryce and Hazlitt often wrote : " Philip was now much safer at Madrid than his grandfather at Paris. All hope of conquering Spain was at an end. But in other quarters the House of Bourbon was reduced to the last extremity. The French armies had undergone a series of defeats in Germany, in Italy, and in the Netherlands. An immense force, flushed with victory, and commanded by the greatest generals of the age, was on the borders of France. Lewis had been forced to humble himself before the conquerors. He had even offered to abandon the cause of his grandson; and his offer had been rejected. But a great turn in affairs was approaching." (Macaulay, *War of the Succession in Spain.*) Such a clipped sentence structure produces a jerky effect. Good plain narrative will flow more easily mingling shorter and longer sentences, the latter not too periodical, whether the scientific period of Merz (p. 41) or the oratorical period of Gibbon or De Quincey, loose sentences if not quite so naïvely loose as the above extracts from Genesis and the *Morte D'Arthur.* One can have too much style in narrative, a statement one might illustrate from Meredith and Stevenson. " The whole secret," says Thomas Hardy, " of a living style, and the difference between it and a dead style, lies in not having too much style—being, in fact, a little careless, or rather seeming to be, here and there. It brings wonderful life into the writing : ' a sweet disorder in the dress, etc.' " This was the fault of the Elizabethan poems, even those of Shakespeare as compared with Chaucer's tales. Chaucer has no rival in our literature as the teller of a good story in a style easy and natural yet with all the dignity which verse requires. Scott is often blamed for the carelessness of his style, but in a piece of narrative he can write excellently : " At last they parted, and my gudesire was to ride hame through the wood of Pitmurkie, that is fou of black firs, as they say. I ken the wood, but the firs may be black or white for what I can tell. At the entry of the wood there is a wild common, and on the edge of the common a little lonely change-house, that was keepit by an ostler wife, they suld hae ca'd her Tibbie Faw, and there puir Steenie cried for a mutchkin of brandy, for he had had no refreshment the haill day. Tibbie was earnest with him to take a bit of meat, but he couldna think o't, nor would he take his foot out of the stirrup, and took off the brandy wholely at twa draughts, and named a toast at each—the first was the memory of Sir Robert Redgauntlet, and might he never lie quiet in his grave till he had righted his poor bond-tenant ; and the second was a health to Man's Enemy, if he would but get him back the pock of siller, or tell him what came o't, for he saw the haill world was like to regard him as a thief and a cheat, and he took that waur than even the ruin of his house and hauld." How Scott can rise as his theme gathers force you may see by turning on in the same tale of the Blind Fiddler to where the hero sees the great bad men of the per-secuting days in, as he believes, hell : " But Lord take us to his keeping, what a set of ghastly revellers they were that sat around that table. . . . There was the fierce Middleton and the dissolute Rothes, and the crafty Lauderdale. . . . And there was Claver-house, as beautiful as when he lived, with his long, dark, curled locks, streaming down over his laced buff-coat, and his left hand always on his right spule-blade to hide the wound that the silver bullet had made. He sat apart from them all and looked at them with a haughty countenance, etc." But it is the first paragraph I took as a good example of the simpler narrative style, which is to my mind preferable to the jerkiness of Macaulay, the eccentricities of Carlyle, even the elegances of Stevenson (see pp. 47-8), though all of these are worth study by one who wishes to write good narrative prose. It is the style of some of the best novelists of to-day, and as ever, one must judge the style in relation to the subject and to the motive of the writer.

It is in the work of the historians who are consciously artists, working in the tradition of Greek and Latin oratorical prose, with many individual variations—Herodotus, Thucydides, Livy, Tacitus —that the paragraph is the important unit logically, emotionally, and sonorously : there that you get the reverberation of which De Quincey speaks. Let us look at Gibbon's account of the final assault on Constantinople, leaving over for the moment the three which lead up to it, of which a word in my next chapter : " The immediate loss of Constantinople may be ascribed to the bullet, or arrow, which pierced the gauntlet of John Justiniani. The sight of his blood, and the exquisite pain, appalled the courage of the chief, whose arms and counsel were the firmest rampart of the city. As he withdrew from his station in quest of a surgeon, his flight was perceived and stopped by the indefatigable emperor. ' Your wound,' exclaimed Palæologus, ' is slight ; the danger is pressing ;

your presence is necessary; and whither will you retire?' 'I will retire,' said the trembling Genoese, 'by the same road which God has opened to the Turks'; and at these words he hastily passed through one of the breaches of the inner wall. By this pusillanimous act he stained the honours of a military life. . . . His example was imitated by the greatest part of the Latin auxiliaries, and the defence began to slacken when the attack was pressed with redoubled vigour. The number of the Ottomans was fifty, perhaps an hundred, times superior to that of the Christians; the double walls were reduced by the cannon to an heap of ruins; in a circuit of several miles some places must be found more easy of access, or more feebly guarded; and if the besiegers could penetrate in a single point the whole city was irrecoverably lost. The first who deserved the sultan's reward was Hassan, the Janizary, of gigantic stature and strength. With his scymetar in one hand and his buckler in the other he ascended the outward fortification: of the thirty Janizaries who were emulous of his valour eighteen perished in the bold adventure. Hassan and his twelve companions had reached the summit; the giant was precipitated from the rampart; he rose on one knee, and was again oppressed by a shower of darts and stones. But his success had proved that the achievement was possible: the walls and towers were instantly covered with a swarm of Turks; and the Greeks, now driven from the vantage-ground, were overwhelmed by increasing multitudes. Amidst these multitudes the emperor, who accomplished all the duties of a general and a soldier, was long seen, and finally lost. The nobles, who fought round his person, sustained, till their last breath, the honourable names of Palæologus and Cantacuzene. His mournful exclamation was heard, 'Cannot there be found a Christian to cut off my head?' and his last fear was that of falling into the hands of the infidels. The prudent despair of Constantine cast away the purple. Amidst the tumult he fell by an unknown hand, and his body was buried under a mountain of the slain. After his death, resistance and order were no more; the Greeks fled toward the city; and many were pressed and stifled in the narrow pass of the gate of St Romanus. The victorious Turks rushed through the breaches of the inner wall; and as they advanced into the streets they were joined by their brethren who had forced the gate Phenar on the side of the harbour. In the first heat of the pursuit about two thousand Christians were put to the sword ; but avarice soon prevailed over cruelty ; and the victors acknowledged that they should immediately have given quarter, if the valour of the emperor and his chosen bands had not prepared them for a similar opposition in every part of the capital. It was thus, after a siege of fifty-three days, that Constantinople, which had defied the power of Chosroes, the Chagan, and the caliphs, was irretrievably subdued by the arms of Mahomet the Second. Her empire only had been subverted by the Latins ; her religion was trampled in the dust by the Moslem conquerors." (Gibbon.)

You could if you wished subdivide that paragraph, stopping for a moment at " the honours of a military life " (I have dropped a sentence on his later career which interrupts the flow of the narrative) ; and again at " irrecoverably lost," " by increasing multitudes," " under a mountain of the slain," and " every part of the capital." For some readers it might help to do so, but it would undoubtedly weaken the effect of the great onward sweep. That you might subdivide is due to the fact that even in this single paragraph Gibbon had to pass to and fro between the two sides which, as we shall see when we touch on the whole composition, is one of the great problems of the narrative writer, be he historian or novelist. In a narrative of a single action it would be more difficult or impossible to subdivide : " Such a gallant line, issuing from the midst of the smoke, and rapidly separating itself from the confused and broken multitude, startled the enemy's heavy masses, which were increasing and pressing onwards as to an assured victory ; *they* wavered, hesitated, *and then* vomiting forth a storm of fire, hastily endeavoured to enlarge their front, *while* a fearful discharge of grape from all their artillery whistled through the British ranks. Myers was killed, Cole, the three colonels, Ellis, Blackeney, and Hawkshawe, fell wounded ; *and* the fusilier battalions, struck by the iron tempest, reeled and staggered like sinking ships. *But* suddenly and sternly recovering *they* closed on their terrible enemies ; *and then* was seen with what a strength and majesty the British soldier fights. In vain did Soult with voice and gesture animate his Frenchmen ; *in vain* did the hardiest veterans break from the crowded columns and sacrifice their lives to gain time for the mass to open out on such a fair field ; *in vain* did the mass itself bear up, and fiercely striving fire indiscriminately upon friends and foes, while the horsemen hovering on the flank threatened to charge the advancing line. *Nothing* could stop that astonishing infantry. *No* sudden burst of undisciplined valour, *no* nervous enthusiasm weakened the stability of their order, their flashing eyes were bent on the dark columns in their front, their measured treads shook the ground, their dreadful volleys swept away the head of every formation, their deafening shouts overpowered the dissonant cries that broke from all parts of the tumultuous crowd, as slowly and with a horrid carnage it was pushed by the incessant vigour of the attack to the farthest edge of the height. *There* the French reserve mixed with the struggling multitude and endeavoured to sustain the fight, *but* the effort only increased the irremediable confusion, the mighty mass gave way *and* like a loosened cliff went headlong down the steep. The rain flowed *after* in streams discoloured with blood, *and* eighteen hundred unwounded men, the remnant of six thousand unconquerable British soldiers, stood triumphant on the fatal hill." The single theme is the advance of the British, for, if for some few sentences the author describes the efforts of the French to oppose that advance, it is only because that is a necessary element in the description of the advance.

There remains description. As I have said earlier, this is one of the most difficult of the tasks of the writer because his medium always in flux has to suggest that of which the parts are co-existent. Bain gives some useful hints for a detailed description if that is what you must attempt. Begin if you can with a general outline. Then, in filling in the details, follow a clearly indicated order consistently throughout. Nothing is more irritating than in a description of a piece of country to find the author now at a town in the north and then at another equally far to the south.

Carlyle was a master of what you might call thumbnail sketches. In the following, of Prague and the valley in which it stands, you get (1) the lie of the city from west to east, and then from north to south ; (2) the course of the valley of the Moldau from the south, across the city, north to the valley of the Elbe :

" Weissenberg is on the hither or western side of Prag : the Hradschin, which is the topmost summit of the city, and of the fashionable quarter,—Old Bohemian Palace, still occasionally habitable as such, and in constant use as a Downing Street,— lies on the slope or shoulder of the Weissenberg, a good way from the top ; and has a web of streets rushing down from it, steepest streets in the world ; till they reach the Bridge and broad-flowing Moldau (broad as Thames at half-flood, but nothing like so deep) ; after which the streets become level and spread out in intricate plenty to right and to left, and ahead eastward, across the river, till the Ziscaberg, with frowning precipitous brow, suddenly puts a stop to them in that particular direction. From Ziscaberg top to Weissenberg top may be about five English miles ; from the Hradschin to the foot of the Ziscaberg, north-west to south-east will be half that distance, the greatest length of Prag city. Which is rather rhomboidal in shape, its longest diagonal this that we mention. The shorter diagonal, from north-most base of Ziscaberg to south-most of Hradschin, is perhaps a couple of miles. Prag stands nestled in the lap of mountains ; and is not a strong place in war ; but the country round it, Moldau ploughing its rugged chasm of a passage through the piled tableland, is difficult to manœuvre in.

" Moldau valley comes straight from the south, crosses Prag ; and,—making on its out-gate at the northern end of Prag (end of ' shortest diagonal ' just spoken of), one big loop, or bend and counter-bend, of horse-shoe shape,—again proceeds straight northward and Elbe-ward. It is narrow everywhere, especially when once got fairly north of Prag, and runs along like a Quasi-Highland Strath amid rocks and hills. Big hill ranges, not to be called barren, yet with rock enough on each hand, and fine side valleys opening here and there. The bottom of your Strath, which is green and fertile, with pleasant busy villages (much intent on water power and cotton spinning in our time), is generally of few furlongs in breadth. And so it lasts, this pleasant Moldau valley, mile after mile on the northern or lower Moldau, generally straight north, though with one big bend eastward just before ending ; and not till near Melnick, or the mouth of the Moldau, do we emerge on that grand Elbe valley,—glanced at once already from Pascopol or other height in the Lobositz times." (Carlyle, *Frederick the Great*).

In the next, also by Carlyle, you get a general sketch of the

Vale of Glamorgan as seen from the town of Llanbethan, and thereafter a number of the features of the Vale without any attempt at arrangement, which is not needed. One might improve here and there, *e.g.* bring the word " a short mile . . . kind of suburb," immediately after Llanbethian.

" Llanbethian hangs pleasantly, with its white cottages, and orchard and other trees, on the western slope of a green hill ; looking far and wide over green meadows and little or bigger hills, in the pleasant plain of Glamorgan ; a short mile to the south of Cowbridge, to which smart little town it is properly a kind of suburb. Plain of Glamorgan, some ten miles wide and thirty or forty long, which they call the Vale of Glamorgan ;—though properly it is not quite a Vale, there being only one range of mountains to it, if even one : certainly the central Mountains of Wales do gradually rise, in a miscellaneous manner, on the north side of it ; but on the south are no mountains, not even land, only the Bristol Channel, and far off, the Hills of Devonshire, for boundary—the ' English Hills,' as the natives call them, visible from every eminence in those parts. On such wide terms is it called Vale of Glamorgan. But called by whatever name, it is a most pleasant fruitful region ; kind to the native, interesting to the visitor. A waving grassy region ; cut with innumerable ragged lanes ; dotted with sleepy unswept human hamlets, old ruinous castles with their ivy and their daws, gray sleepy churches, with their ditto ditto, for ivy everywhere abounds ; and generally a rank fragrant vegetation clothes all things ; hanging in rude many-coloured festoons and fringed odoriferous tapestries, on your right and on your left, in every lane. A country kinder to the sluggard husbandman than any I have ever seen. For it lies all on limestone, needs no draining ; the soil, everywhere of handsome depth and finest quality, will grow good crops for you with the most imperfect tilling. At a safe distance of a day's riding lie the tartarean copper forges of Swansea, the tartarean iron forges of Merthyr ; their sooty battle far away, and not, at such safe distance, a defilement to the face of the earth and sky, but rather an encouragement to the earth at least ; encouraging the husbandman to plough better, if he only would."

It is not always possible to use the different quarters, north, south, etc., to indicate directions. But you may frequently begin

with either the foreground or the background and work *in* towards
the one or *out* towards the other :

> And one a *foreground* black with stones and slags,
>   *Beyond*, a line of heights, and *higher*
> All barr'd with long white cloud the scornful crags,
>   And *highest*, snow and fire.

That is a picture by Tennyson which in the first version of the
poem, *The Palace of Art*, had been the rather confused attempt
which follows :

> And one a foreground black with stones and slags,
>   Below, sunsmitten icy spires
> Rose, striped with long white cloud the scornful crags,
>   And highest, snow and fire.

Compare in the same way the first and the final versions of the
description of the valley at the beginning of *Oenone*. I can give
only the final version. Note that you are supposed to be looking
towards Troy with the hill Gargarus behind your back :

> There lies a vale in Ida, lovelier
> Than all the valleys of Ionian hills.
> The swimming vapour slopes athwart the glen,
> Puts forth an arm, and creeps from pine to pine,
> And loiters, slowly drawn.   On either hand
> The lawns and meadow-ledges midway down
> Hang rich in flowers, and far below them roars
> The long brook falling through the clov'n ravine
> In cataract after cataract to the sea.
> Behind the valley topmost Gargarus
> Stands up and takes the morning : but in front
> The gorges, opening wide apart, reveal
> Troas, and Ilion's column'd citadel,
> The crown of Troas.

Or look at Scott's description of Edinburgh and the country
beyond as seen from Blackford Hill (*Marmion*, canto iv. 30).

But to follow an accumulation of detail is for a reader very
difficult. One is very apt to skip descriptions in novels. In the
modern drama they are generally wisely confined to a few important positions—doors, windows, etc. In a serious prose work

you are best, if it can be managed, to supplement with a map or plan. In poetry the wiser method is to give, well described by the best epithet or epithets, some of the characteristic features and then leave to the reader to fill in the scene from his own memory and imagination. Few of us but in childhood have seen the Crucifixion on some hill resembling one familiar to ourselves. Gray thus indicates the coming of evening : " The curfew tolls the knell, etc." Keats's *Ode to Autumn* is a masterpiece of such description. In the first stanza are given a selection of features : misty skies, ripe fruit, nuts, bees gathering honey that suggest the close of summer, its final perfection. In the second he passes on to the later phase of the ingathering—the winnower, the reaper, the gleaner, the ciderpress, at the same time indicating by the transfiguring effect of personification, the quickening of his own feeling. In the last stanza we have autumn trembling on the verge of winter : the barred clouds, the stubble-fields, and the sounds :

> the small gnats mourn
> Among the river-sallows, borne aloft
>   Or sinking as the light wind lives or dies :
> And full-grown lambs loud bleat from hilly bourne ;
> Hedge-crickets sing ; and now with treble soft
> The red-breast whistles from a garden-croft ;
>   And gathering swallows twitter in the skies.

Each reader will fill in the picture from his own imagination and memory. The genius of the poet is seen in his selection and the accurate epithets, including verbs. Each stanza is a paragraph.

I have suggested, as a useful exercise, the close examination of any paragraph in your reading, especially if it strikes you as difficult to follow : (1) taking each sentence by itself, (2) then in its relation to that which precedes and that which follows, and (3) taking the paragraph as a whole and asking if the emphasis is well distributed. This may lead to a complete reconstruction of the paragraph, or even the breaking of it up into more than one. What follows is a paragraph from one of Bain's examination papers :

The abolition of monarchy and the introduction of plural or republic government, which had its origin in Greece, was both a proof of the high intelligence of the Greeks, and a powerful auxiliary in the subsequent advancement of their civilisation. It was at first an effect, and afterwards became a conspiring cause, of their superiority to the Asiatic nations, to the nations which they designated as *barbarian*. The Greeks were the inventors of corporate government, of the system of dividing the sovereign power among a number of co-ordinate persons, whose combined assent was necessary to an act of the supreme authority. For this assent of the sovereign body unanimity was not requisite : it could be given by the majority. This system was invented by the Greeks, as much as the pendulum clock was invented by Huygens, or the steam-engine by Watt. When it was introduced by them, the world had known nothing but monarchy. It is the essence of a free government : without the distribution of the sovereign power among a body, free government cannot exist. This important principle in the art of government the Greeks conceived clearly, and after a time they applied it universally in their small city communities. The office of the ancient hereditary king was either abolished, or converted into a sacerdotal dignity ; any individual, who, by cajoling or intimidating the people, was able to make himself a *tyrant*, or despot, was regarded as an usurper, and his rule rested on force. The Greeks detested the usurped and illegitimate government of one man, but their application of the principles of corporate government was unskilful. They either divided the entire sovereignty among a few men, determined by birth or wealth, or they divided it among the entire free body of citizens. The former government was called an oligarchy or aristocracy, the latter a democracy. There was no contrivance for delegating the sovereign power, as in the modern system of Political Representation. In an oligarchy, the oligarchs were independent of popular election ; in a democracy, the entire people exercised their sovereign rights directly, and without appointing any representatives to act for them. This unskilful application of an invaluable principle produced two ill results in the republics of antiquity, one with respect to their internal, the other with respect to their external relations. As to their internal relations, the ruling body in an oligarchy was too independent of the people, while the ruling body in a democracy was too numerous for intelligent government, and was liable to be stimulated to passionate decisions by eloquent demagogues. As to their external relations, they were unable to incorporate conquered territory into their own system of government, upon fair and equal terms. A newly acquired province became a dependency, under the ruling body of citizens in the sovereign state. Nevertheless, with all their defects, the free government of France and Italy produced all that was precious in antiquity—their literature, their art, their science, their history. It was through them

that the foundations of our modern European civilisation were laid.
They were a necessary condition for the existence of a state of society and
education which could not grow up under the Oriental system of
monarchy; the most improved method of government which the
Greeks found in being.

I have endeavoured to reconstruct as follows :—

" The abolition of monarchy and introduction of plural or republican
government, which became so powerful an auxiliary in the advancement
of their civilisation, a cause of their superiority to the Asiatic nations,
the nations which they designated as barbarians, was a striking proof
of the high intelligence of the Greeks.   Corporate government, the
system of dividing the sovereign power among a number of co-ordinate
persons, whose combined assent—unanimity was not requisite, it could
be given by a majority—was necessary to the act of the supreme authority,
was invented by the Greeks as much as the steam-engine was invented
by Watts or the pendulum-clock by Huygens.   Before its introduction
by the Greeks the world had known nothing but monarchy, the con-
centration of sovereignty in one person.   But corporate government is
the essence of free government ; without the distribution of the sovereign
power among a body free government cannot exist.   This is the
important, the vital principle which the Greeks were the first to apprehend
clearly.

" Conceiving it clearly, the Greeks soon applied the principle
universally in their small city-communities.   The office of the ancient
hereditary king was either abolished or converted into a sacerdotal
dignity.   Any individual who, by cajoling or intimidating the people,
was able to make himself a tyrant or despot was regarded as a usurper
whose rule rested on force ; and such usurped, illegitimate government
of one man was detested.

" But while they thus clearly apprehended, and firmly maintained, the
principle of corporate government, their application of the principle was
unskilful.   They either divided the entire sovereignty among a few
men, determined by birth or wealth, or they divided it among the entire
free body of citizens.   The former government was called an oligarchy
or aristocracy, the latter a democracy.   There was no contrivance for
delegating the sovereign power, as in the modern system of Political
Representation.   In an oligarchy the oligarchs were independent of
popular election ; in a democracy the entire people exercised their
sovereign rights directly, and without appointing any representative to
act for them.

" This unskilful application of an invaluable principle produced two evil results in the republics of antiquity, one with respect to their internal, the other with respect to their external relations. As to their internal relations, the ruling body in an oligarchy was too independent of the people, while the ruling body in a democracy was too numerous for intelligent government, and was liable to be stimulated to passionate decisions by eloquent demagogues. As to their external relations, they were unable to incorporate conquered territory into their own system of government upon fair and equal terms. A newly acquired province became a dependency under the ruling body of citizens in the sovereign state. Nevertheless, with all their defects, the free government of Greece produced all that was precious in antiquity—their literature, their art, their science, their history. It was through them that the foundations of our modern European civilisation were laid. They were a necessary condition for the existence of a state of society and education which could not grow up under the Oriental system of monarchy—the most improved method of government which the Greeks found in being."

Bain gave later a version of his own, in *On Teaching English* (1887) :

" Before the Greeks, the world knew of no other Government besides monarchy ; to them exclusively was owing the introduction of plural or republican government ; the system of dividing the sovereign power among a number of co-ordinate persons whose combined assent, as given by the majority, was necessary to an act of supreme authority. This is the essence of free government ; without the distribution of the sovereign power among a body, free government cannot exist. Detesting the usurped and illegitimate government of one man, and clearly conceiving the benefits of the corporate system, the Greeks after a time applied it universally in their small city communities. The office of the hereditary king was either abolished, or converted into a sacerdotal dignity ; and any individual who, by cajoling or intimidating the people, was able to make himself a tyrant or despot was regarded as an usurper and his rule rested on force. There was, however, a want of skill in the carrying of the corporate principle into practice. Either the entire sovereignty was divided among a few men, determined by birth or wealth, or else it was exercised by the whole body of the free citizens. The first of the two methods was called an oligarchy, the second a democracy. Their defects were these : in an oligarchy the oligarchs were independent of popular election ; in a democracy the entire people exercised their sovereign rights directly ; for both these defects representation would have been the remedy," etc., etc.

The rest as it stands, for neither of us suggests any change in the last sentences.

To me, I confess, Bain's version, if clearer than the original, has sacrificed to clearness too much of the force and dignity which, despite its faults, the original does to my mind have.

CHAPTER VIII

THE WHOLE COMPOSITION

A well-constructed plot, therefore, cannot either begin or end at any point one likes. . . . To be beautiful a living creature, and every whole made up of parts, must not only present a certain order in its arrangement of parts, but also be of a certain definite magnitude. Beauty is a matter of size and order, and therefore impossible either (1) in a very minute creature, since our perception becomes indistinct as it approaches instantaneity; or (2) in a creature of vast size—one, say, 1000 miles long—as in that case, instead of the object being seen all at once, the unity and wholeness of it is lost to the beholder. Just in the same way, then, as a beautiful whole made up of parts, or a beautiful living creature, must be of some size, a size to be taken in by the eye, so a story or plot must be of some length, but of a length to be taken in by the memory.—Aristotle: *Poetics*, ch. vii.

ARISTOTLE is here speaking of the plot of a tragedy, and I hope to be able later to consider what he here states in that definite connection. But I have taken the quotation here as an indication of an effect that you may aim at in many different kinds of composition, in works of very different size. It is an additional satisfaction if in an essay or a book you can feel at the end not only that you have derived pleasure from this or that part of the work, or this or that special feature—the language, the character-drawing, the thoughts, the descriptions—but that as you lay it down you have the impression of a single directing purpose throughout, a theme which has been worked out to the end, or what you are prepared to accept as an end, a story with a beginning, a middle, and an end. Even a work as large as Gibbon's *Decline and Fall of the Roman Empire* does give you that impression as you lay it down and look back on all that you have learned from different chapters of the book—the succession of emperors good or bad, the various barbarian invasions, the growth of the Christian religion, etc., etc. The principles which we have seen to govern the construction of the sentence and the paragraph are equally valid for the work as a whole—coherence and the right distribution of the emphasis as determined by the purpose you have in view. We have taken the sentence first, and this is the order you will follow from the minute you put your pen to paper. But before you do put pen to paper you must proceed in the opposite order. You must sketch, at least in your mind, the general plan of your work, and get some idea of the order in which you mean to proceed. You may find as soon as you have got under way that you have made a false start, and must begin over again; or you may find that your general plan is correct but needs some modification of what you had expected to be the order in which you would proceed. The transitions will be the important thing for yourself and for your reader. Stop every now and then and read over what you have written to see if you, putting yourself in the place of the reader, can follow the passage from paragraph to paragraph clearly, and that in an order which you can further develop without misleading the reader.

Consideration of the order you are to follow takes us back to the division I made in a previous chapter, a division which arises out of the fundamental division of our experience—the flow of events in time, the relative position of things in space, the sequence of ideas in the mind as determined by what seem to us rational connections (take a proposition in Euclid as a good example of such a sequence) or as dictated by the association of ideas or images in the mind when endeavouring to give expression to an emotional mood. Compare with a proposition of Euclid the order of thoughts or images in a lyrical poem such as Wordsworth's " Behold her single in the field," or Shelley's *Skylark*, if there be a definite order in the latter.

Of the three main divisions which we made according to the above classification of our experiences—narrative, description, exposition—I propose to begin with the last (on each I can attempt no more than to give some intelligible hints and to refer you to some good models), because it covers so many varieties, from a purely scientific or philosophic essay by Hume or Darwin or Huxley, etc., through an oration aiming at persuasion, to a piece of prose or verse whose sole aim is to communicate a mood of mind.

In my last chapter I suggested your taking to exemplify the paragraph a paragraph of a predetermined length. Now there are, and have been since Petrarch wrote, many sonnet-sequences. Such sequences by no means always consist of sonnets following one another in a connected narrative or argument. More often they are series of sonnets harping independently on the same main theme and could be rearranged without harm to the meaning of any one of them. But sometimes such a narrative or argument does connect several of them thus closely. I will take three such from Shakespeare's sonnets to his friend. In the first of them he declares that in his friend's love he has everything he can desire; but he may lose this if his friend desert him. No, says the next, for with the loss of that love life for him would end; but perhaps his friend will be false to him without his knowing the truth; for, says the third, his friend's beauty will make it impossible for him to detect any falsehood:

> Some glory in their birth, some in their skill,
> Some in their wealth, some in their body's force;
> Some in their garments, though new-fangled ill;
> Some in their hawks and hounds, some in their horse;
> And every humour hath his adjunct pleasure,
> Wherein it finds a joy above the rest:
> But these particulars are not my measure;
> All these I better in one general best.
> Thy love is better than high birth to me,
> Richer than wealth, prouder than garments' cost,
> Of more delight than hawks or horses be;
> And, having thee, of all men's pride I boast:
>   Wretched in this alone, that thou mayst take
>   All this away, and me most wretched make.

> But do thy worst to steal thyself away,
> For term of life thou art assured mine;
> And life no longer than thy love will stay,
> For it depends upon that love of thine.
> Then need I not to fear the worst of wrongs,
> When in the least of them my life hath end.
> I see a better state to me belongs
> Than that which on thy humour doth depend:
> Thou canst not vex me with inconstant mind,
> Since that my life on thy revolt doth lie.
> O! what a happy title do I find,
> Happy to have thy love, happy to die!
>   But what's so blessed-fair that fears no blot?
>   Thou mayst be false, and yet I know it not.

> So shall I live, supposing thou art true,
> Like a deceived husband; so love's face
> May still seem love to me, though alter'd new;
> Thy looks with me, thy heart in other place:

> For there can live no hatred in thine eye,
> Therefore in that I cannot know thy change.
> In many's looks the false heart's history
> Is writ, in moods and frowns and wrinkles strange;
> But heaven in thy creation did decree
> That in thy face sweet love should ever dwell;
> Whate'er thy thoughts or thy heart's workings be,
> Thy looks should nothing thence but sweetness tell.
>   How like Eve's apple doth thy beauty grow,
>   If thy sweet virtue answer not thy show!

Three sonnets follow elaborating in different ways the main thought of the evil effect of vice being hid in a beautiful mansion.

I have taken these three sonnets to illustrate, without too great length, first, the unity of thought in each, though in the two first the last line ushers in a new thought which becomes the subject of the next; secondly, they suggest the somewhat measured way in which you should develop an argument making sure of each step. In most early essays the young writer, in my experience, passes too quickly from one point to another. His paragraphs consist of a few lines. As the farmer complained of *Johnson's Dictionary*, he changes the subject too often. I do not wish you to make the paragraph too long; but it must develop the subject fully enough to make the reader pass on prepared and interested to the next. Look back to the paragraph which I gave at p. 40 from Merz's *A History of European Thought in the Nineteenth Century* (1896-1914), and study again the care with which, even by repetitions (repetitions which have a different purpose in view from Shakespeare's), he endeavours to make his meaning quite clear before he goes on to what is to follow. Or take any good expository essay in our prose since Johnson: Hume, Adam Smith, Macaulay, Arnold, Newman, Shaw in his prefaces. The argument moves on from paragraph to paragraph more or less quickly or slowly according to the requirements of the subject and the audience.

Working, then, in paragraphs, in what order will you develop the whole? In the *Rhetoric*, Aristotle divides a speech aiming at persuasion into four main parts—the exordium, the narrative and proof, in that order but often interwoven, and finally the peroration: "I never like to interrupt a young speaker," said Disraeli in replying to a savage attack, " especially when I see him approaching his peroration." [1] This rather formal order is the more necessary in a speech inasmuch as your audience must go with you the whole time. They cannot turn back as in reading to recover whatever they may have missed ; but it is not a bad order to keep in mind in shaping an essay. The way in which you will use the opening or exordium and the end or peroration depends again on your audience and the end you have in view. If you are addressing or writing for a specialist audience, like, for example, a bench of judges in the Chancery Courts or a society of scientific experts, then your address will be to the intelligence, and the opening is used to best advantage in a sketch of what you are to try and establish by argument or evidence : " To justify us in taking the administration of their affairs out of the hands of the East India Company, on my principles, I must see several conditions. First, the object affected by the abuse should be great and important ; second, the abuse affecting this great object ought to be a great abuse ; third, it ought to be habitual, and not accidental ; fourth, it ought to be incurable in this body as it now stands constituted. All this ought to be made as visible to me as

[1] All that Aristotle has to say about the parts of a speech (book iii, chapters xiii, xiv—use Welldon's translation) is interesting and amusing if you read carefully, for his style is very condensed, and study his examples so far as they are available, adding examples from our own literature. Most of his examples are taken from the poets. In a speech addressed to an intelligent, specialist and unprejudiced audience there should be just two parts in a speech, the statement of what you are to prove and the proofs. But in addressing more popular audiences you must excite interest, combat prejudices and, it may be, awaken prejudice against your opponent. Hence the importance of the exordium and the peroration. For example, if you wish to combat a prejudice which has been excited against you or your client or your cause, that should come in at the very outset. But if you wish to excite prejudice against your opponents, then this should be your closing charge, your peroration, " that they may be more easily remembered." If in appealing to your audience you must often dwell on the importance of the subject, there are times when it is better to make them inattentive by conveying the impression that the subject is really of no such importance as has been maintained. In an " epideictic " or complimentary speech it is well sometimes to begin with an apparent irrelevance which amuses your audience and then to link it cleverly with the main subject : " It may be added that such a flight of the orator into a new region has the pleasing effect of relieving the uniform character of the speech."

the light of the sun before I should strike off an atom of their charter " (Burke, *Fox's East India Bill*).

But if you are speaking to a more or less popular audience, of whose interest and attention you cannot be sure, then the exordium will be used, at least in part, to quicken their curiosity and attention by dwelling on the importance of the subject or its special interest for the audience in question : " As I am persuaded, Athenians, that you are convened now about affairs of greatest moment, such as affect the very being of the state, I shall endeavour to speak of them in the manner most agreeable to your interests " (Demosthenes, the *Fourth Philippic*). " Depend upon it this business cannot be indifferent to our fame. It will turn out a matter of great disgrace or great glory to the whole British nation. We are on a conspicuous stage, and the world marks our demeanour " (Burke, *Fox's East India Bill*, for changes in the government of India). Our orators do not often strike so high a note. " We meet in a time of great stress, when events are moving very fast and no final views can easily be taken. I have thought to tell the House about the great battle in Egypt which has been a British victory of the first order, and also about the other half of the combination, namely of the United States and British intervention in North Africa " (Winston Churchill). In like manner, according to your audience and purpose, you will use the peroration either to sum up clearly what you maintain you have proved, or you will use it for a fresh appeal to the interest and feelings of your hearers : " You have now heard truths of the highest moment urged with all freedom, simplicity and zeal. You have heard a speech not filled with flattery, danger and deceit ; calculated to bring gold to the speaker, and to reduce the state into the power of enemies. It remains, therefore, that the whole tenor of your conduct be reformed ! If not, that utter desolation which will be found in your affairs must be imputed wholly to yourselves " (Demosthenes, *op. cit.*). Compare with this the close of Burke's speech *On Conciliation with America*, his faith in, and glorification of, the spirit of the British Constitution. But you are not likely to be called on to address such august audiences on so high themes. Look, then, rather at the opening and close of an essay by Macaulay or Carlyle, and if I mention these authors often it is not that I recommend them as final models. Each has definite and at times trying tricks, but among these are devices for securing lucidity and giving emphasis to what they wish to drive home. You may employ their methods in a quieter way and compare them with authors whose methods are more subtle. Macaulay loves an effective opening : " We doubt whether any name in literary history be so generally odious as that of the man whose character and writings we now propose to consider " (on Machiavelli). But Macaulay was an orator and writes generally as an orator. Other essayists open more quietly, often in an indirect way, as it were at a little distance from the proper subject, which is also, of course, a way of stimulating interest, expectation. But, as in the sentence and the paragraph, it is the end which is the importantly emphatic place. The beginning may startle ; it is the end which drives home. Matthew Arnold opens a lecture on Milton by commenting on the Anglo-Saxon tendency, especially as seen in America, to disparage supreme excellence, to think that " excellence was common and abundant. But excellence is not common and abundant." So he works on to the supreme excellence, among English authors or poets, of Milton as an artist : " In the sure and flawless perfection of his rhythm and diction he is as admirable as Virgil and Dante, and in this respect he is unique among us. No one else in English literature and art possesses the like distinction." That becomes Arnold's theme and leads up to the close which at once emphasises this theme and broadens our view of its significance : " Milton has made the grand style no longer an exotic here ; he has made it an inmate amongst us, a leaven, and a power. Nevertheless he, and his hearers on both sides of the Atlantic, are English, and will remain English—

Sermonem Ausonii patrium moresque tenebunt.

The English race overspreads the world, and at the same time the idea of an excellence the most high and the most rare abides a possession with it for ever."

You will begin an expository essay, then, by either outlining what you are to expound or prove, or in some way interesting your audience, awakening expectation. The narrative and proof which follow may be taken in order or interwoven. An example of the former is the speech in which, for example, the Agent for the Crown states what is the Crown's theory of the crime which they will undertake to prove by witnesses. In his final speech he will bring together the evidence and attempt to show that the Crown's theory has been established. But in a less formal essay you will generally find that the statements and relevant proofs are taken step by step together. Your great aim will be to carry your reader on from paragraph to paragraph in a logical, persuasive order. At the end you will sum up or in some way make impressive what you have developed. Of course, in a quite informal, talkative essay you will purposely avoid too great an appearance of pedantic system. Look at an essay by the French essayist, Montaigne, or by Lamb on borrowers and lenders, or some such fantastic subject. Read in order to learn to write yourself. Examine every sentence in a paragraph to see if you could improve the position of those clauses which may be moved about, could make the coherence and emphasis better. Do the same then with the paragraph. In sentence, paragraph, and essay the same rule holds, the same stars are your guides—coherence and emphasis, the latter determining how you will begin and how you will end.

But as I have said, exposition is not always logical. Your order is sometimes determined by the way in which one sentence suggests another, not by logic but by association. The extreme case is a lyric, not a ballad where a story is told. Wordsworth, while discussing the diction proper to poetry, touches on this question of order : " The end of poetry is to produce excitement, an unusual and irregular state of mind ; ideas and feelings do not in that state of mind succeed each other in an accustomed order." What happens is that the thoughts succeed each other by an often apparently casual connection. What gives unity to the whole is that these thoughts are all appropriate to a single dominant mood of feeling. Take Burns's *Mary Morison*. I will divide not as the verses are divided for the music, to be sung, but as the thoughts are distinct from one another :

> O Mary, at thy window be,
>   It is the wish'd, the trysted hour,
> Those smiles and glances let me see
>   That make the miser's treasure poor !

> How blithely wad I bide the stour,
>   A weary slave frae sun to sun,

Could I the rich reward secure,
  The lovely Mary Morison.

Yestreen when to the trembling string
  The dance gaed through the lichted ha',
To thee my fancy took its wing,—
  I sat, but neither heard nor saw,
Though this was fair, and that was braw,
  And yon the toast of a' the toun,
I sigh'd, and said amang them a',
  "Ye are'na Mary Morison."

O Mary, canst thou wreck his peace
  Wha for thy sake wad gladly dee?

Or canst thou break that heart o' his
  Wha's only faut is loving thee?

If love for love thou wilt na gie,
  At least be pity to me shown;
A thought ungentle canna be
  The thought o' Mary Morison.

The thoughts are frequently more closely connected, for instance
in the *Solitary Reaper* of Wordsworth:

Behold her, single in the field,
Yon solitary Highland lass.

The thought of the girl's voice is more dominant throughout. But
there is no reasoning, the connections are all emotional, *e.g.*
comparisons:

A voice so thrilling ne'er was heard
In spring-time from the cuckoo-bird,
Breaking the silence of the seas
Among the farthest Hebrides.

A hyperbole, of course, evoked by the feeling of the poet, like
the very fanciful reference to the nightingale in the preceding lines.
Then, as quite naturally when anything interests us deeply, comes
the question. One would know more about it:

Will no one tell me what she sings?

and then as the feeling subsides he returns to the girl and himself listening :

> The music in my heart I bore
> Long after it was heard no more,

which last line is said to have suggested the whole poem. But a strain of reasoning *can* come into a lyric which is the expression of feeling. Look back to the sonnet by Donne, quoted on p. 116. Feeling does so quicken thought. In Donne's lyrics, as well as the sonnets proper, there is this effect of a succession of thoughts not arising from casual resemblances or associations, but springing from a process resembling reasoning. Look at *The Good Morrow* and note the way in which he follows up the fancy of lovers being one and inseparable. Donne has had considerable influence on modern poets, yet not, it seems to me, in this direction. The peculiarity of many modern lyrics is that they have carried still farther the tendency to let the mind follow casual, often merely personal, associations. What are the links binding the thoughts in the following, and what the dominant feeling ?

> I sang as one
> Who on a tilting deck sings
> To keep their courage up, though the wave hangs
> That shall cut off their sun.
>
> As storm-cocks sing
> Flinging their natural answer in the wind's teeth,
> And care not if it is waste of breath
> Or birth-carol of spring.
>
> As ocean-flyer clings
> To height, to the last drop of spirit driving on
> While yet ahead is land to be won
> And work for wings.
>
> Singing I was at peace,
> Above the clouds, outside the ring :
> For sorrow finds a swift release in song
> And pride its poise.
>
> Yet living here
> As one between two massing powers I live,
> Whom neutrality cannot save
> Nor occupation cheer.

None such shall be left alive :
The innocent wing is soon shot down,
And private stars fade in the blood-red dawn
Where two worlds strive.

The red advance of life
Contracts pride, calls out the common blood,
Beats song into a single blade,
Makes a depth-charge of grief.

Move then with new desires ;
For where we used to build and love
Is no man's land, and only ghosts can live
Between two fires.

Only the poet himself could tell us exactly what thoughts were racing through his head. A reader may guess, or feel, that he is comparing his life in a civilisation which is dying to the song of one who knows he must perish, a flyer who knows he cannot reach land, the storm-cock of a ship heading for some unknown country ; thereafter the thought grows more personal and obscure.

In narrative writing the course is pretty clear if you have only the one line to follow, to relate the experiences of a day, or of a year in the life of one man (it may be yourself), of a year in the history of a country. What you have chiefly to look out for are, first, that you do follow the order of events consistently, not turning back and forward and so puzzling your reader ; second, how to deal with digressions, for at times you will come on some name of a person or a place of whom or which you are aware the reader will need further information. If this is likely to take up space, the best thing will be to start a new paragraph intimating that it is a digression from which you will return after a time. If it is a small but necessary thing you wish to state, you can use a device which writers rather like but readers generally do not—add a note at the foot of the page.

Serious difficulty begins when you have to tell a story which involves two or more simultaneous series of events. It is then you have to consider at what point you must break off from one of these and bring another up to the same date. As Carlyle says, " an historian must write so to speak in lines ; but every event is a superficies, nay, if we search out its causes, a solid." Look at Gibbon's account of the fall of Constantinople, from which I have quoted one paragraph at pp. 118-9. In three preceding paragraphs you get in the first an account of the preparations on the Turkish side. In the next on the side of the Christians in the city : " Far different was the state of the Christians." Then comes the general assault followed by the paragraph which I quoted ; and so on. Gibbon gives to each paragraph a heading in the margin indicating its theme, not a bad device for oneself and the reader. In a similar account of the Battle of Waterloo, there would be more than two threads to bring together. You might begin with a description of the opening of the battle from the British side, the first assaults of the French cavalry. Then as the day wears on and it becomes clear that the first assaults are not to break at once the British defence, you might pass to the French side and show what has determined the course of the battle under Napoleon's direction. Finally, as the combat becomes more and more dubious and both leaders grow anxious, it will be necessary to digress in order to relate the doings of the French army under Grouchy and the German army under Blucher. It is the arrival of the latter on the field that leads to the final French assault, their repulse and the *sauve qui peut*.

Coming to imaginative narrative—ballad, lay, drama, epic poem, novel—you are met with the question of plot interest. Not every historian dealing with actual events has taken the trouble of Macaulay or Carlyle to make the telling exciting, Macaulay giving you the same kind of interest you might get from reading the daily papers during a political crisis ; Carlyle picturing the events as vividly as a good film might. A serious student of history will not be put off by some dryness in the narration. Grote, for example, or Hallam, or the *Cambridge Modern History* make no such attempt. You may take or leave them is their point of view. But who is going to read a dry or dull account of events that never happened ? An elderly friend of my youth gave me once to read a history of how events should have gone in England if Charles I. had won a righteous victory. I could not get far in it ; but on the other hand, for a serious student of history there might be, and indeed was, interest in the imaginary account by G. M. Trevelyan (a grandnephew of Macaulay) of what would have been the condition of England and Europe for some years if Napoleon had been victorious at Waterloo. If you are to be interested in an imaginary story you must find in it some positive quality, something exceptional in the character of the events as in *Robinson Crusoe* or *Gulliver's Travels*, interesting imaginary characters, beauty of language and thought, as, for some people at any rate, in *Marius the Epicurean*. But one great means of awakening and sustaining interest is the plot, the interest of suspense, the desire of the audience or reader to know what will happen. When Alexandre Hardy came to Paris as a dramatist he found that the audiences in the theatre would not listen to the well-written plays of the imitators of Seneca and classical drama, but preferred the crude Spanish melodramas with their surprising turns in events. There may be other interests as well, character and style, but even character is best brought out by action, the part played in the development of the plot. Are there, then, different kinds of plot ? That there are is clear from the names Comedy, Tragedy, Romance. Let us look at some of them.

One obvious and recurrent type is what I will call the romantic plot, the story of a " wish-fulfilment." In this the characters who are intended to awaken your chief interest and sympathy are exposed to difficulties and dangers from which in the end they emerge safe and happy, often to the sound of marriage bells. Aristotle and Bain both give interesting hints on the story or plot. You must keep up the suspense, not give away the solution. The detective story is the favourite kind of plot of this kind at present, though here again some writers can combine with the plot-interest good drawing of character. Earlier examples are *Big Claus and Little Claus*, *Cinderella*, *Tom Jones*, etc. In the detective story you are not necessarily made to wish for one conclusion rather than another. But in the more serious story or novel, aiming at a fuller picture of life, your interest is enlisted at once or gradually for the chief characters, what are called the hero and heroine, and you watch with increasing interest what will happen to them. We are on the side of Tom Jones or David Copperfield, or Emma, or whoever it may be. It is not necessary that you should approve of all that the hero does. One good variety of plot is that in which the hero outgrows his own failings, is schooled and disciplined by life, and shapes for himself an at least tolerably happy end to the story. David Copperfield does so to some extent, and Arthur Pendennis. George Meredith was specially fond of this type of plot and tried to trace the deeper elements in the character, which gradually develop. The same is true of his chief contemporary, George Eliot. If it is less common in modern novels it is because the novelist is on his guard to avoid anything like a moral interest, what might be accounted didactic.

These are the two chief interests of the romantic plot, when plot is to be a chief interest. Some minor suggestions for supporting the interest of expectation are given by both Aristotle and Bain. Episodes which postpone the solution, especially if they are of a kind that suggest a different end from what you had begun to expect, quicken suspense. But the two essentials of a convincing story are that the solution come about at once naturally, and yet so as to surprise ; naturally, that is, without the intervention of what was called a *deus ex machina*, the sudden death of a wealthy uncle or the discovery that one is a long-lost heir. But indeed few stories would progress without some element of chance. Life is full for all of us of unexpected coincidences. Aristotle is clear as to the two requirements, probable evolution (δι᾽ εἰκότων) and surprise, which he thinks is best secured by two devices, what he calls ἀναγνώρισις and περιπέτεια, generally translated " recognition " and " revolution." " A peripeteia is the change from one state of things within the play to its opposite, and that too in the way we are saying, in the probable or necessary sequence of events " ; (as it is, for instance, in the *Œdipus* of Sophocles) ; " here the messenger who comes to gladden Œdipus and to remove his fears as to his mother, reveals the secret of his birth " (cap. xi ; see the whole). An obvious example is the speech of Portia in the trial of Antonio which seems to be leading straight to the victory of Shylock (" A Daniel come to judgment ! yea, a Daniel ") and ends in his complete and shattering defeat :

> A Daniel, still say I ; a second Daniel !—
> I thank thee, Jew, for teaching me that word.

By recognition, *anagnorisis*, is meant the discovery who someone really is, which discovery alters the whole state of affairs: Iphigenia's discovery that the stranger whom it is her duty to sacrifice is her brother Orestes, the discovery in *Guy Mannering* that Brown is the lost heir, etc. As stated by Aristotle in the *Poetics*, they seem to be just two of the tricks by which you may enliven a tragedy. But the *Poetics* represent probably only short notes of what Aristotle had taught. Mr F. L. Lucas, in his interesting and valuable book, *Tragedy* (The Hogarth Press, 1927), has shown how much more there is in Aristotle's contention; the deepest tragedy is that in which the destruction is the work of, is brought about by, your own or your friends' efforts to secure some quite different purpose, the very opposite : " The most poignant tragedy of human life is the work of human blindness—the Tragedy of Error " (Lucas, *op. cit.*, p. 93). But of tragedy again.

The romantic plot is the most common, for the very good reason that most readers prefer a happy ending. It may be, and is, the truth that a tragic story moves us more deeply, and we may later consider why, though our primary concern is simply that of plot-construction. To be able to compose a moving tragedy or an amusing and impressive romance or comedy is not something that can be taught. All that a teacher can do is to suggest how to overcome some of the difficulties that may be encountered in getting the tragic story across in the form of drama or novel. Before, therefore, going on to other kinds of plots one may here touch on some other points to bear in mind besides those mentioned —creating suspense, awakening sympathy with one side in the dramatic conflict, protracting and complicating the element of suspense. There remains the difficulty of getting started, letting your audience or readers into the position of affairs from which your particular story begins. The simplest but clumsiest way is by an introductory chapter or narrative. Scott was too apt to be content with this, but even Shakespeare does not always avoid it, *e.g.* in *The Tempest* where, after a brief scene describing the shipwreck, Prospero informs Miranda at length, and thereby the audience, of how he comes to be on the island, and who they are that are now by his art brought to that island and there wrecked but with no loss of life. As some critic observes, it is little wonder that Miranda falls asleep, though this is, as a fact, due to her father's art. In the *Odyssey*, and in imitation of the *Odyssey* in the *Æneid*, the poet adopts a method which Horace in the *Ars Poetica* converted into a rule, and which Milton follows. You plunge *in medias res*—Æneas and his companions wrecked on the coast near what was to be Carthage (that has a significance which does not belong to the main story but to the later history of Rome), Satan and his host prostrate on the floor of hell. Then later you find an occasion on which the hero or another can narrate the events which have led up to the opening situation. You can, of course, do the same in a novel. Sometimes in a play you start with a conversation which lets you tell the main facts in a natural way. Make some study of the openings of Shakespeare's plays or, to come nearer home, of Ibsen, who is a master of construction.

And now for a word on comic and tragic story or plot. I say story or plot (*mythos*) because there may be tragic and comic incidents and scenes in a story or plot which is itself romantic. The troubles pass, the comic scenes are incidental. The persons for whom your main sympathies have been engaged are left happy, or as happy as life permits. At the end of Plato's *Symposium* the imaginary narrator of what happened at the feast tells how, when the rest of the company had either gone home or fallen asleep, he found on awakening himself that Socrates, Aristophanes and Agathon—the philosopher, the comic poet, and the tragic poet (who had just gained the prize for his first tragedy)—were still " drinking out of a large goblet which they passed round, and Socrates was discoursing to them, Socrates insisting to the other two that the genius of comedy was the same as that of tragedy, and that the writer of tragedy ought to be a writer of comedy also." What all Socrates had in view in this contention I do not know. Those to whom he maintained the paradox were " compelled to consent, being sleepy, and not quite understanding his meaning." But the remark is not irrelevant to this question of plot, for the comic and the tragic plot both differ from that of romance, and resemble one another. Romance ends in victory. Our main wishes as regards the hero or heroine or both are fulfilled. Both tragedy and comedy end in defeat, though the defeat is of a different kind in each and leaves us with a different feeling. In a tragic story, whatever form it take, ballad, epic, drama, or novel, your interest and sympathy are enlisted for certain people as in a romance, but what the story develops is their defeat, the disaster which overtakes them, it may be their death—Agamemnon, Œdipus, Hamlet, Lear,

Clarissa, Tess. In the comic story, of which the dominant interest is the story, you are shown some character or characters who in one way or another awaken your contempt, dislike, or it may be hatred, and you witness their overthrow, see them exposed and defeated—Big Claus defeated by Little Claus. This is the general character of the carefully hammered out comedies of Ben Jonson, of the more skilfully and wittily elaborated comedies of Molière. Shakespeare in the drama and Dickens in the prose novel prefer a romance for the main plot, but the victory of the hero often involves the defeat of a Shylock, a Malvolio, a Pecksniff, etc. The defeat is at times of too serious a character to awaken laughter or even ridicule of a crueller kind. The fate of the villain, Ralph Nickleby, or Goneril and Regan may in itself be tragic, but it is not as tragic as the fate of Macbeth or Lear is, because our interest is not in them but in the victim who has escaped. From their fate if tragic we tend to turn away our eyes. " Cover their faces ! " And sometimes feelings change with the progress of the centuries. There has been a tendency in critics, as Lamb and his followers, to pity Shylock and Malvolio, and even Falstaff, so magnificently turned off by the young Prince when the hour has come to throw off his loose behaviour and

> Pay the debt I never promised.

It is the habit just now to attribute this tendency to the romantic strain in criticism. It may be due to a growth in humane feeling. Savages laugh at a drowning man, if he is not of their tribe. Jane Austen in some of her stories unites the comic and romance effects in the same person in a delightful manner, *e.g.* Emma. As a matchmaker Emma is sadly defeated when she discovers that she has encouraged her friend to fall in love, or think that she has fallen in love, with the man whom Emma herself loves, the great Mr Knightley. But the defeat opens her eyes to the state of her own heart and all goes well in the traditional romantic manner.

But the deepest note in literature is the tragic. The note of tragedy runs through all great literature from the beginning. " The ballad," says the late W. P. Ker, " has no fondness for the happy ending, which is generally right in the fairy-tale. The tragic motive is as common in the ballads as in the older heroic

L

poetry, and the modern Greek name for a ballad, *tragoudi*, might be taken for those of other languages. The best of them are lyrical tragedies" (*Form and Style in Poetry*, London, 1928). Think of *Sir Patrick Spens, The Bonny Earl of Murray, Fair Margaret and Sweet William, The Braes of Yarrow, Lord Randall, Fair Annie*. What is true of the ballad is true, the same critic declares, of the epic. Romance deals in adventures and there may be adventures in epic, even comic scenes (like the quarrels of the gods), but the interest of the adventures is subordinate to the interest we take in the tragic fate of Sigurd and Hildebrand and Roland and Hector and Achilles. " From Homer," said Goethe, " I every day learn more clearly that in our life here above ground we have strictly speaking to enact Hell." For a study of the mystery of our enjoyment of tragedy you cannot begin better than with the visit of Priam to Achilles to recover the body of his son Hector : " ' For his sake have I come unto the ships of the Achæans, that I may win him back from thee, and I bring with me untold ransom. Yea, fear thou the gods, Achilles, and have compassion on me, even me, bethinking thee of thy father. Lo, I am yet more piteous than he, and have braved what none other man on earth hath braved before, to stretch forth my hand toward the face of the slayer of my sons.' Thus spake he and stirred within Achilles desire to make lament for his father. And he touched the old man's hand and gently moved him back. And as they both bethought them of their dead, Priam for man-slaying Hector wept sore, as he was fallen before Achilles's feet, and Achilles wept for his own father and now again for Patroclus, and their moan went up throughout the house. But when noble Achilles had satisfied himself with lament . . . he sprang from his seat and raised the old man by his hand, pitying his hoary head and hoary beard, and spake unto him winged words and said : ' Ah, hapless ! many ill things verily hast thou endured in thy heart. How dost thou come alone to the ships of the Achæans and to meet the eyes of the man who slew full many of thy brave sons ? Of iron verily is thy heart. But come, then, seat thee on a seat and we will let our sorrows lie in our hearts, for all our pain, for no avail cometh of chill lament. This is the lot the gods have spun for miserable men, that they should live in pain ; yet themselves are sorrowless. For *two* urns stand upon the floor of Zeus, one filled with his evil gifts, and *one* with blessings. To whomsoever Zeus . . . dealeth a mingled lot, that man chanceth now upon ill and now again upon good, but to whom he giveth but of the bad kind him he bringeth to scorn, and evil famine chaseth him over the goodly earth, and he is a wanderer honoured of neither gods nor men. . . . Keep courage and lament not unabatingly in thy heart. For nothing wilt thou avail by grieving for thy son, neither shalt thou bring him back to life or ever some new evil come upon thee.' " There is the tragic position unrelieved. No *hamartia* is dragged in, whether that of the men who are suffering or of some remote ancestor of the human race, so as to justify the ways of the gods to men. This is their way and we must bear it, but the human heart can endure—" Nathless he so endured."

But such arraignment of the gods as the source of all the tragic happenings in the " sad history of our race " could not satisfy the religious mind, and the Greeks were a very religious people, though our familiarity with the intenser feeling and the mono-theism of the Hebrews makes us at times forget the fact. A little study of Greek history will show how much importance the Greeks attached to discovering the will of the gods by oracle and sacrifice, how unwilling they were to neglect, even for military reasons, the established festivals in honour of this or that god. Even in the passage that I have cited Priam hints that the gods do not approve of wanton cruelty : " Yea, fear thou the gods, Achilles." Later, Plato will exclude from his republic Homer's tales of the doings of the gods. But before we come to Plato we must consider the Greek tragedians who, in their way, try to moralise the tragic stories. One way of clearing the gods was to take the blame upon ourselves, the sufferer, whence later Aristotle's doctrine of the *hamartia* : " There are three forms of plot to be avoided. (1) A good man must not be seen passing from happiness to misery, or (2) a bad man passing from misery to happiness, . . . nor on the other hand should (3) an extremely bad man be seen falling from happiness into misery. Such a story may arouse the human feeling in us, but it will not move us either to pity or to fear ; pity is occasioned by undeserved misfortune, and fear by that of one like ourselves ; so there will be nothing either piteous or fear-inspiring in the situation. There remains, then, the intermediate kind of personage, a man not pre-eminently virtuous and just, whose misfortune, however, is brought about not by vice and depravity but by some error of judgment, of the number of those in the enjoyment of great reputation and prosperity, *e.g.* Œdipus, Thyestes, and the men of note of similar families." Leaving out this last reference to the kind of families, of great men who were accepted by Greek tragedians as suitable heroes, we may ask how the consciousness of the calamity being due to an error of judgment (as Bywater here understands *hamartia*) or some moral fault, some misdeed for which, as Saintsbury used to put it, there is infinite excuse but no final justification, how this affects our feelings. Bacon thinks that it makes the tragic sentiment deeper, because it leaves the sufferer without anyone whom he may blame, another man or the gods : " Then all strikes deadly inward and suffocateth." But Aristotle and those who have welcomed the doctrine of the tragic error as justifying providence have generally taken it as making of the disaster a punishment, a punishment indeed often out of all proportion to the fault, which is not easy to accept as justice. " Suppose he err'd ; it is not the intent of God or man, to hunt an error so to the death with a revenge beyond all measure and proportion " (Milton, *Tetrachordon*). But (1) it is clear that in exact proportion as the calamity seems to take the character of just punishment does it lose the character of tragedy. It is the something more, the to our eyes *undeserved* element of suffering, the mysterious element, that constitutes the tragic. (2) It is obviously quite impossible to find a definite *hamartia* if that be taken as meaning moral fault to account for the tragic fate of many of the most famous characters of extant tragedy, Greek or English. What of Antigone, or Desdemona, or Cordelia, or Hippolytus, or many another ? And this has been always so obvious that the Greek tragedians, at least Æschylus, sought for the *hamartia* further back, in the family : " Æschylus," says Jebb, " treated the story of Œdipus as he treated the story of Agamemnon. Œdipus becomes the foremost figure of a trilogy which traced the action of an inherited curse in the house of Labdacus, even as the Oresteia traced the action of such a curse in the house of Pelops." The Jews, not in the Old Testament apparently, but in the interval between that and the New, laid all the blame for human suffering on the father of the race, and St Paul took this over as the nucleus of his Christian theology. But the Jews did not write tragedies ; nor have the Chinese nor the Indians admitted the type of drama which ends in complete and undeserved disaster. That seemed to them to cast a slur on the ways of Providence ; and so it seemed to Dr Johnson. He thought it was the duty of the dramatist, a duty which Shakespeare too often shirked, to show at the end a proper distribution of justice. He tells us that he was so shocked by King Lear's death and that of Cordelia (not justified even by Shakespeare's sources) that he could never read the drama again till he had to edit the play. So strong is this feeling among unsophisticated readers to-day that Hardy had to alter the conclusion of *Tess* when that story appeared in periodical form. Tragic drama was a Greek creation. But into all the problems raised by the enjoyment in drama or fiction of what we should shrink from in reality I must not attempt to go here. Read such studies as *Tragedy*, by W. Macneile Dixon (London, 1924), and writers touched on there, as Nietzsche, Hume, Hegel, and others. For my purpose, which is just to distinguish different types of plot and indicate some of the factors which seem requisite in each, it will suffice to lay down that (1) a tragedy deals with the disastrous fate of some character or characters in whose fortunes you are made to be deeply interested, even if as in *Macbeth* you are not asked to admire them or to condone their actions ; (2) the suffering must not appear as though it were the entirely just punishment of some fault, there must at least be more in it than that ; but on the other hand to make, as in some of Hardy's novels, the hero or heroine the helpless, undeserving victim of circumstances is equally disturbing to the proper effect of tragedy ; (3) in some way or other you will compensate for the suffering portrayed by (*a*), among perhaps other things, the greatness of the characters who suffer (in *Macbeth* it was not the fate of Duncan or Banquo which moved the present writer when he saw it performed by Barry Sullivan some sixty years ago, the first drama he ever witnessed ; it was Macbeth and Lady Macbeth, their suffering throughout culminating in, for Macbeth, the scene when he entered with the words " I have done the deed," and pointing to his hands, cried, " This is a sorry sight," and all that follows, and for Lady Macbeth, in the sleep-walking scene) ; (*b*) the touches of

philosophy, criticism of life, that the great poet weaves in ; and
(c) the beauty of the verse and style. Beauty must be the final effect.
Aristotle stresses pity and fear. But pity and fear may be awakened
by a story of the sufferings of people without a spark of greatness.
We may pity them, but, as Carlyle described his own feeling, it
may be pity mingled with abhorrence and contempt. In the
tragic hero, even if involved in crime, there must be something
great, something that produces

> sorrow that is not sorrow but delight,
> And miserable love that is not pain
> To hear of, for the glory that redounds
> Therefrom to humankind and what we are.

Defending the drama against the criticism of such Fathers as
Tertullian and Cyprian and Lactantius, to say nothing of many
of his Puritan contemporaries, Milton writes : " Quid enim in
tota philosophia aut gravius aut sanctius aut sublimius tragœdia,
quid utilius ad humanæ vitæ casus et conversiones uno intuitu
spectandos ? " ; " For what in the whole of philosophy is more
impressive, purer or more uplifting than a noble tragedy ? What
more helpful to a survey at a single glance of the hazards and
changes of human life ? " But not the least factor in the final
effect is the beauty of the form—diction, imagery, thought, rhythm,
and a harmony in which the most diverse elements are combined
to produce the final effect of beauty, that mysterious but all-
convincing experience :

> Beauty : the Vision whereunto,
>   In joy, with pantings, from afar,
> Through sound and odour, form and hue,
>   And mind and clay, and worm and star—
> Now touching goal, now backward hurled—
> Toils the indomitable world.

Finally, the degree to which the plot constitutes the dominant
interest in drama or novel differs very much from writer to writer.
To the Elizabethan dramatist, even to some extent to Shakespeare,
the individual scenes are the chief consideration ; hence the possi-
bility of two or more dramatists collaborating. The same is true
of some novels, notably those of Sir Walter Scott. In French
tragedy, on the other hand, Corneille, and more perfectly Racine,

developed a concentrated story in which every scene, every speech has a bearing on the development of the surprising catastrophe, but this is achieved, not as in a detective story by surprising happenings, but by subtle moral reasoning in Corneille, by the fluctuating course of passionate feeling in the heart of a man or more often of a woman in the drama of Racine. But for a further study and classification of plots see Edwin Muir, *The Structure of the Novel* (Hogarth Press, 1928).

GENERAL INDEX TO TOPICS

Arguments (" topics ") : kinds of, intellectual, moral, emotional, 5-11

Audiences : kinds of, 11-12, 16-17, 20

Composition :

(a) Sentence, guiding principles of idiomatic or grammatical correctness, 94-97 ; order of words as determined by usage and by regard for coherence and the right distribution of emphasis, 93-105 ; examples from different authors, 105-112 ; rhythm as enforcing the importance of the end of the sentence, 112-114

(b) Paragraph : importance of good paragraphing, 115 ; sonnet as an example of paragraph 116 ; types of, expository 117-119 ; argumentative, 119-120 ; narrative, 120-126 ; descriptive, 129 ; the critical study of, 130-134

(c) the whole composition : order of, Aristotle's divisions of a speech, 138-139 ; different ways of opening an expository speech or essay, 139-142 ; order in a lyrical poem not logical, 142-145 ; order in narrative, difficulties involved, 120-126 ; in description, 126-130 ; plot in imaginative narrative, its importance, interest of suspense, 146-147 ; types of plot : romantic, the happy ending, 147-150 ; comic and tragic, defeat in both but differently presented and felt, 150-157

Figures of Speech : what they are and the laws of mind on which they depend for their effect, 54-57 ; the purpose they serve in the communication of feeling by their contribution to (a) vivid objectivity of description and (b) imaginative transfiguration, 59-79

Oratory : kinds of, 6-7, 15-16 ; relation to poetry, 17-21 ; subject-matter, 21-23 ; purposes of, 24-27

Poetic Diction : wider and narrower senses of, 82-83 ; Aristotle's classification of words available for the poet, 83-84 ; some varieties of in the history of English poetry, 85-92

Style : varieties of, 40-52 ; " colour " of words as a factor in, 29, 33-35, 36-38 ; " plain " style, " decorative," " grand," 44-52 ; dependence on diction, imagery, sentence structure, harmony and rhythm, 54-55

Words : qualities of, 28-31 ; Campbell's classification of, 32-35 ; propriety in the use of, its relative character, 35-39

SOURCES OF THE CHIEF PASSAGES QUOTED

Chapter I. p. 1, Milton : *Paradise Lost*, IX, 665-78. p. 3, Cicero : *De Oratore*, II, 30. " Nam et apud eos dicimus qui nesciunt, et ea dicimus quae nescimus ipsi." p. 8, Burke : *Two Letters to Gentlemen in Bristol*, *Works* III, 218f.

Chapter II. p. 16, Hobbes's *Leviathan*, Part I, Chap. 11. " And therefore Eloquent speakers are enclined to Ambition ; for Eloquence seemeth wisdom both to themselves and others." Abbé Huvelin : *Some Spiritual Guides of the 17th Century*. p. 17, Swift: *Journal to Stella*. Mill : On *Poetry* in *Dissertations and Discussions*. pp. 17-19, Keble : *De Poeticae Vi Medica*, Lectures on Poetry, Oxford, 1832-41 ; tr. E. K. Francis, 1912. The translation in the text, however, is my own. p. 19, Nietzsche : *The Birth of Tragedy ;* Keats : *Fragment of an Ode to Maia ;* Shelley : *To Jane : The Invitation.* p. 20, Swinburne : *Songs Before Sunrise.* p. 21, Byron : *Childe Harold*, IV, xcviii. p. 26, Wordsworth : *Preface to Lyrical Ballads*, Second Edition.

Chapter III. p. 31, Quintilian : *Institutes of Oratory*, tr. J. S. Watson (1888), Bk. VIII, Chap. I. p. 32, Campbell : *Op. cit.* Bk. II, Chap. I. p. 40, Cicero : *Ad Marcum Brutum, Orator*, especially XI 37-XXVIII 100. Before coming to oratory, speech intended to persuade, Cicero touches on the style (1) of the philosopher which, with exceptions such as Plato, is what I have called colourless : " mollis est enim oratio philosophorum et umbratilis, nec sententiis nec verbis instructa popularibus, nec vincta numeris (not over rhythmical), sed soluta liberius ; nihil iratum habet, nihil invidum, nihil atrox, nihil miserabile, nihil astutum ; casta, verecunda, virgo incorrupta quodam modo. Itaque sermo potius quam oratio dicitur," etc. ; (2) the style of the historian ; (3) of the sophist (what we might call the stylist pure and simple, intent on display, etc.) ; (4) of the poet, more rhythmical, though prose can be rhythmical, and in his diction allowed a greater licence. Coming then to oratory he finds three styles (1) the plain (" subtile "), which he describes in detail much as in my text. It looks an easy style to master, but is not, for though not colourful it has juice (" habeat tamen sucum aliquem oportet "), does not cultivate rhythm, uses current words, is sparing of figures, and these homely, does not follow too studied an order, etc. ; (2) a style which stands midway between this and the highest : " Uberius est aliud aliquantoque robustius quam hoc humile, de quo dictum est, summissius autem quam illud de quo iam dicetur." This I have treated as the decorative, but there is overlapping ; (3) " Tertius est ille amplus copiosus gravis ornatus in quo profecto vis maxima est," etc. (xxviii). The great orator is he who knows how to blend the three, " qui poterit parva summisse, modica temperate, magna graviter dicere." p. 41, Merz, *op. cit.* II, pp. 167-70. p. 44, Reynolds : *Discourses*, ed. Gosse, 1883 ; especially the fourth. The grand style is represented by " the Roman . . . the Florentine, the Bolognese

schools " and " the best of the French school, Poussin, Le Sueur and Le
Brun " ; the decorative or ornamental by the Venetians, excepting Titian.
The plain style (though Reynolds does not make a third class) might
from what he says of them be represented by " the painters of the Dutch
school." p. 47, The Countess of Carberry's Funeral Sermon in *Works*, ed.
The Rev. Charles Page Eden, M.A., 1854, vol. viii, p. 447. p. 48, Stevenson :
Travels with a Donkey ; Gray : *On A Distant Prospect of Eton College ;*
Tennyson : *In Memoriam*, closing section. pp. 50-1, Bright : Speech
during the Crimean War. p. 51, " Lay not, etc.," *Hamlet*, III, 4, 145f.

Chapter IV. p. 54, " But he, etc." Cowper : *Table Talk.* p. 56, " Our two
souls, etc.," Donne, *A Valediction ; forbidding mourning.* p. 58, " Yes !
in the sea, etc." Arnold : *To Marguerite—continued.* Compare the
same poet's *Human Life.* Sophocles : *Philoctetes*, II, 785-6, but see
throughout. Jebb translates, " Ah me, oh, oh, thou hapless foot, what
torment wilt thou work to me ! " p. 59, Quintilian, *op. cit.* Bk. VIII,
Chap. iii. p. 60, Browning, *The Flight of the Duchess.* p. 62, Tennyson :
Locksley Hall, and Kipling : *Gentlemen Rankers.* p. 63, Scott : *Lady
of the Lake*, Canto V. p. 64, " Nigh upon that hour, etc.," Tennyson,
Gareth and Lynette ; " Bluff Harry, etc.," Tennyson, *The Talking Oak ;*
" Blind mouths," *Lycidas*, 119. One of Milton's daring synecdoches.
Compare from *Samson Agonistes :*

> A thousand foreskins fell, the flower of Palestine
> In Ramath-Lechi famous to this day.

pp. 65-6, Homer : *Iliad* B., 87f, tr. Lang, Leaf and Myers. p. 66, Milton :
Paradise Lost, I, 768f. Browning : *Up at a Villa—Down in the City.*
" I never heard, etc." Sidney : *Defense of Poesy.* " Love is flower-like, etc.,"
Coleridge : *Youth and Age.* " For I am, etc.," Byron : *Childe Harold*,
III, 2. Burns : *Man Was Made to Mourn.* p. 67, " But why o' death, etc."
Burns : *Epistle to James Smith.* " The tomb is now, etc." Carlyle : *Sartor
Resartus*, Book II, Chap. 3, and Book III, Chap. 10.. pp. 68-9, Keats :
The Eve of St Mark. pp. 69-70, Milton : *Paradise Lost*, I, 300f. p. 70,
Hazlitt : *My First Acquaintance with Poets*, *Works*, vol. 8, p. 14. p. 71,
Rossetti : *The Blessed Damozel.* pp. 72-3, Shakespeare : *The Merchant
of Venice*, III, 2, 47f ; *Macbeth*, V, 5, 18f. p. 74, Psalm cxiv, " When
Israel went forth out of Egypt." Horace : *Odes*, I, 14. Scott : *Marmion*,
Introduction to Canto V. p. 75, Marlowe : *Dr Faustus.* Burke : *Reflec-
tions on the French Revolution.* Shakespeare : *Macbeth*, II, 2, 61-4.
p. 76, Burns : " *My love*, etc." Shakespeare : *Othello*, V, 2, 337-355 ;
my attention was first drawn to this, as irony used to express a grief too
great for words, in a lecture by Arthur Sidgwick at Corpus Christi College,
Oxford. p. 77, Pope : *Essay on Criticism*, 693-6.

Chapter V. p. 80, Rossetti : *The Blessed Damozel.* *Hudibras* II, ii, 31-2.
Tennyson : *The Brook.* p. 81, Chaucer : *The Nonne Priestes Tale.* Spenser :
Epithalamion. p. 83, Logan Pearsall Smith : *Words and Idioms*, 1925.
p. 91, " Or where, etc." Tennyson : *In Memoriam*, X ; " And half-cut-
down," etc. Tennyson, *Audley Court*, 25-28. p. 92, *Paradise Lost*, III,
32f. Goethe : *Torquato Tasso*, I, 2, 66-7.

Chapter VI. p. 100, To this list of Grammars add *The Grammarian and His
Material*, by J. M. Wattie. The English Association, Pamphlet No. 75.
The writer does not accept Jespersen's view that spoken English gives

the norm for correct grammar : " the grammarian has to seek for an account of the ellipses of spoken English . . . by a reference to the real standard, which is contained in the great corpus of English Literature." p. 103, 1 Corinthians xiii. 1-4. p. 106, Goldsmith : "On Abuse of Our Enemies," *The Public Ledger*.[1] Addison : *The Spectator*, No 37, April 12, 1711. pp. 108-9, Swift : *Gulliver's Travels, Voyage to the Houyhnmns*. p. 110, Macaulay : *Milton* (August 1825, in *Edinburgh Review*). That on Ranke's *History of the Popes* was written fifteen years later, October 1840. p. 111, Tennyson : *The Charge of the Light Brigade ; Locksley Hall*. Such bold inversions, like certain figures, imply a heightened mood of feeling and are to be used in prose with caution : " Pleasant, as the fiery heat of the desert daylight is done, is our homely evening fire"; "Delightful now was the green sight of Teyma, the haven of our desert." Doughty : *Arabia Deserta*. pp. 111-12, Carlyle : *The French Revolution*, Book V, Chap. 9. p. 113, Dickens : *Dombey and Son*, Chap. 1. p. 114, Milton : *Animadversions upon the Remonstrant's Defence against Smectymnuus*, Sect. IV. Burke : On Fox's East India Bill.

Chapter VII. p. 116, Shakespeare : *Sonnets*, cxvi. Donne : *Holy Sonnets*, viii. p. 117, Arnold : Introduction to *Ward's English Poets*, 1883 ; reprinted in *Essays in Criticism*, Second Series, 1888. pp. 119-20, H. J. Laski : *Liberty in the Modern State*, Cambridge. pp. 120-1, Genesis, xxviii. 10-15. p. 121, *Morte D'Arthur*, I, 28. p. 122, " The whole secret, etc," *The Early Life of Thomas Hardy*, by F .E. Hardy, p. 138. pp. 122-3, Scott : *The Blind Fiddler's Tale*, in *Redgauntlet*. pp. 123-5, Gibbon : *Decline and Fall of the Roman Empire*, Chap. lxviii. p. 125, Napier's *History of the Peninsular War*, Book V, The Battle of Albuera. pp. 126-7, Carlyle : *Frederick the Great*, XVIII, Chap. 2. p. 128, Carlyle : *John Sterling*. Part I, Chap. 3. pp. 130-2, I have failed to discover whence Bain took this extract.

Chapter VIII. pp. 137-8, Shakespeare : *Sonnets*, xc, xci, xcii. pp. 144-5, Cecil Day Lewis : *The Conflict* in *Overtures to Death*. p. 144, "I sang as one . . . their"; not strictly correct. Compare, however, " If ye forgive not everyone his brother their trespasses," etc. Poutsma, *op. cit.*, gives other modern examples. pp. 151-2, W. P. Ker : *op. cit.*, p. 25. pp. 152-3, Homer : *Iliad*, xxiv. tr. Lang, Leaf and Myers. pp. 153-4, Aristotle : *Poetics*, cc. 14-16. See *Aristotle : On The Art Of Poetry, Translated by Ingram Bywater, with A Preface By Gilbert Murray*, 1920. p. 156, " Sorrow that is not, etc." Wordsworth : *Prelude*, XIII, 246f. " Beauty : the Vision, etc.," William Watson : *The Father of the Forest*.

---

[1] Reprinted in *The Works of Oliver Goldsmith*, ed. Peter Cunningham, Vol. III, pp. 331-2.

PRINTED IN GREAT BRITAIN BY OLIVER AND BOYD LTD., EDINBURGH